TellTale Souls Writing the Mother Memoir

"Rarely does a book carve out a unique place for itself within the hallowed halls of writerly advice and wisdom, yet Ms. Henriksen has fearlessly stepped into uncharted, original waters with *TellTale Souls Writing the Mother Memoir*. Not only is this a book for me to recommend to the many people interested in writing their own story, but one to keep on my desk as a reference tool to inspire my writing moments. *TellTale Souls* brings to mind both *Writing Down the Bones* by Natalie Goldberg and *Walking on Water* by Madeleine L'Engle. It is destined to be one of the classics required to complete the journey for writing the truth and writing it well. I've discovered a new favorite that incorporates all the aspects of writing I trust and believe in— spirituality, memory, passion, and the power of story!"

—River Jordan, author of *Praying for Strangers: An Adventure of the Human Spirit*

"*TellTale Souls* is an inspired guide for those who want to explore the loving but complex emotional terrain that exists with our mothers. With gentle encouragement, Henriksen invites us to journey into our pasts, skillfully laying bare the nature of memory itself. An eloquent exploration of creativity and memory for writers and non-writers alike."

—Zoe FitzGerald Carter, author of *Imperfect Endings: A Daughter's Story of Love, Loss and Letting Go*

"'Emotional memory' is as universal as mothers. Lynn Henriksen helps writers and would-be writers explore the far reaches of their emotional memories along with the more tangible, sensory memories to create stories, essays or poetry. In her beautifully designed and organized "how-to write a powerful memoir" book, she artfully guides the writer through the dark mazes of the heart, illuminating them with the power of the imagination."

—Talia Carner, author of *Jerusalem Maiden, China Doll, and Puppet Child*

"Memoir is tricky business. It requires allegiance to the truth and, at the same time, the ability to craft a compelling story. Questions arise: How to access memory? What is important? What about sequencing? Where it the borderline of fiction? Through *TellTale Souls Writing…* Lynn Henriksen dissects the idea of memoir into its many invisible parts and shows us a framework for making it all come together. She gives activities, prompts, examples and if we worry the process is becoming too mechanical, passes along advice as to how to go about accessing the deepest spiritual truths. In the end, and with her guidance, we might not only make literature out of memory but be blessed with unexpected enrichments of spirit."

—H. David Watts, M.D., author of *Bedside Manners* and *The Orange Wire Problem and Other Tales from the Doctor's Office*

"Every writer should read this book, as its combination of the spiritual and the practical transcends other memoir writing guides. The gifted Lynn, a lyrical, perceptive writer and teacher, brings incisive advice and technique together with true stories for a carefully devised, matchless performance, in which the reader will play a major part. I wish I had read *TellTale Souls* years ago; it would have saved me a lot of trouble. It is a tour de force and bound to become a classic."

—Ann Seymour, author of *I've Always Loved You: A True Story of WW2 in the Pacific battlefields, in California, and in the Imperial Palace, Tokyo*

"'To run after a shadow and learn to describe it…' For those of us who long to capture our mothers' spirits in words (and who among us doesn't?)—that's exactly how writing a mother memoir feels. Happily, we have a mentor and companion in Lynn Cook Henriksen's *TellTale Souls*. Part can-do, part how-to, this book leads us along a writer's path rich with prompts and exercises, hints and watchwords. Inspirational sources illuminate every step of the way with illustrative vignettes written by all kinds of people about all kinds of moms. Their stories trigger ours. Through guided exploration, we discover (and chronicle!) the depths and truths of our mothers' lives."

—Amanda McTigue, author of *Going to Solace*

"In five tenderhearted acts, Lynn Cook Henriksen creates a stage from real life, a theater in the round centered around our mothers, and guides us in an open ended approach to write a lasting impression of Mother through story. Along the way we are delightfully instructed through a sampling of authentic and unforgettable memoirs, vignettes, and poems. Henriksen is encouraging, never dictating, and suggests a variety of techniques and exercises to bring our own memories of Mother into an enduring literary form."

—Kate Farrell, editor of *Wisdom Has a Voice: Every Daughter's Memories of Mother*

"As caring a writer as she is a daughter, author and speaker, Lynn Henriksen has developed a matchless method to help every daughter and son keep their recollections of mother vivid and fresh through *Writing the Mother Memoir*. Her brilliant technique, explained in clear and compassionate terms and alive with true stories, is simple to follow even if one is not a writer by trade. I highly recommend this guidebook."

—Patricia V. Davis, bestselling author

"Tell Tale Souls Writing the Mother Memoir is a gentle guide that invites you to explore the terrain of mother-child relationships, a journey of wisdom, courage, and heart. In every chapter you'll discover tips and techniques that invite you to breathe life into stories about your mother and times gone by. This book is a true memoir writer's companion."

—Linda Joy Myers, Ph.D., author of *The Power of Memoir, How to Write Your Healing Story*

TELLTALE SOULS

——WRITING——

THE MOTHER MEMOIR

TELLTALE SOULS

——WRITING——

THE MOTHER MEMOIR

How to Tap Memory and Write Your Story
Capturing Character & Spirit

Lynn Cook Henriksen

Indigo Roads Press

Published in the United States of America by Indigo Roads Press.

Cover design by Brenda Duke, San Francisco, CA.

Library of Congress Cataloging-in-Publication Data
Henriksen, Lynn Cook.
Telltale souls writing the mother memoir: how to tap memory and write your story capturing character and spirit / Lynn Cook Henriksen / 1st ed.
Includes glossary of literary terms and definitions.

ISBN 978-0-9850559-4-3 (pbk)

2012935839

Creative Writing • Memoir • Women's Studies / Indigo Roads Press, Tiburon, CA.

In memory of you,
my mother and muse, Margaret "Midge." I feel
your dazzling spirit shining through
everything I do.

To my family and friends for their patience, belief
in my work, and sustaining encouragement; especially my
sister for being there every time and always from
the beginning of this journey.

For all TellTale Souls I've come to know in incomparable ways
as you trusted me with glimpses of your mothers' spirits, I thank you. For
those TTS whose Mother Memoirs didn't tie in with
the lessons in this book, please know I've plans for
them, too—they will be shared.

CONTENTS

Contents

AUTHOR'S NOTE

The purpose of this book is to move you beyond thinking about writing memoir to actually writing memoir of a special kind, the *Mother Memoir*. The significance will be realized as you achieve success by journeying through the Five Acts comprising this guide. My aim is not to keep you in suspense about what I mean by the *Mother Memoir*, but, rather than be repetitious, I thought it best to explain it fully and only once in Act One since there are readers, believe it or not, who skip over author notes and introductions.

We find memoir of some type at most every turn—from books and screen plays; workshops and classes; blogs and magazine articles; to advice on how, where, and why to publish memoir, along with techniques on how to preserve stories as keepsakes within families.

Memoir is a hot topic today; although, to my knowledge, nothing new in the use of technique or focus has come on the scene to shake things up until now with this direct focus on how to write the *Mother Memoir*. While reiterating age-old principles, I will introduce you to a method for writing memoir with a distinct and refreshing difference.

There is a central intent inherent in the act and art of memoir writing, and there are reactions and thoughts generated by and around it that encompass all types of memoir, from autobiographical and biographical stories and family legacy to travel musings and spiritual revelations, to name just a few subsets of this genre. When people begin to contemplate writing personal narrative, even when they passionately want to tell their stories, the very idea of it can be overwhelming; thoughts of it are fraught with doubt about whether or not they have the skills they perceive necessary to write stories others will embrace. Challenging questions float through their consciousness about where to begin and end, which memories to include, and which to lay aside. They wonder if bringing certain buried memories and touchy subjects into the light of day will be too painful for them to contemplate or too difficult for their families to read, or they are uncertain whether they can find the words to convey their feelings through a story that means so much to them—and will anyone, other than themselves, care about what they have to say.

As you make your way through this book, you will discover a distinct framework through which to find the answers to your questions, as well as a unique view for approaching memoir that will unfold before you with a spirited and giving dimension. You will explore how to get in touch with memories rife with hidden possibilities and be encouraged to open yourself up, through writing, to truths previously trapped by old tapes running and rerunning through your thoughts without mindful or spirit-seeking interaction. As you express yourself through this writing process, you will come to see new perspectives and depths of understanding that will fulfill you and give your characters the life they deserve and your story genuine pizzazz.

For years, my heart was the guide I used to help people on this particular journey into understanding and writing the *Mother Memoir*. When the prospect of continuing to lend my heart out like a library book began to seem slightly ridiculous, I decided to write this book, which will stand in an exciting niche all its own. My goals for this book are to show you how to make writing memoir a realistic accomplishment, to lead you on a spiritual quest, and to take the mystery out of tapping memory and writing memoir by instilling a belief in you that you are the only one who can tell the stories you need to tell in the way you want them told. I give you activities to coax memory and writing tools to stimulate the creative process as you unravel the complexities of intimate relationships and personal experiences while writing from your heart. This guidebook is a result of years engaging with people individually, teaching memoir classes and workshops, and listening to and responding to cues from my students, friends, and fellow writers. Active involvement, for well over a decade, in the *Mother Memoir* realm by writing *The Story Woman* blog, editing bio-vignettes, granting interviews, and answering myriad questions, has given my work the edge I sought.

This book is complete with prompts, exercises, and telling tales. It is filled with tips and food-for-thought for writers of any level. To notch-up and add reality to the how-to aspect, I have strategically interlaced short, true stories from successful writers of the *Mother Memoir* throughout this guided journey.

Trust in this—you do have what it takes to write. The memories and the know-how are there inside you waiting to be aroused. As you work your way through this book, my belief is that you will become as passionate as I am about the value of discovering personal truths, often buried deep. When that happens, and it will, intimate knowledge can be yours if you pay attention to an internal and universal rhythm.

The writers I have come to know tell me their time spent on this journey brings joy, sometimes sorrow, it was frequently poignant, often cathartic, and always stimulating. From my experience in helping hundreds of people write the *Mother Memoir*, I feel comfortable promising you that if you take to heart what you read throughout this guide and follow the exercises and writing prompts you will find the truths you are seeking. Through this experience, you will find the voice that is distinctly yours by which to tell your stories confidently.

From the start, I invited people into my world of memoir by showing them the way to write true tales illuminating the spirit of their mothers in just a few character-grabbing pages. This made the act of writing memoir doable. Now I am welcoming you to follow that path and accomplish your goal of writing an important story; although it may signal the threshold to longer works, it is, most definitely, a significant end in itself.

Through my desire to help people write true tales that depict the spirit of their mothers and then to bring their voices together to share these intimate slices of life, I have chosen forty stories from my collection and strategically placed them throughout the book to give you real-life, down-to-earth connections. Taken together, the short memoirs will give you glimpses of the variety of ways mothers mother, while at the same time, they will show you that at their core, mothers are mothers are mothers the world over.

Writers and readers now have an avenue to connect through compassion and understanding, learn from one another, and rejoice in our "oneness." This assemblage of characters rings clear with the genuine voices of a wide range of people who write with an authenticity born of heart and soul.

Walking this creative path with you is a privilege.

Thank you,
Lynn

Act One

You are Hereby Invited into the Heart of

the World of the Mother Memoir

Come along with me. Be my guest on a journey of discovery. As a TellTale Soul, it's often been said, you'll slip and you'll slide on emotions that erupt from deep places. You'll meet extraordinary characters who dwell in curious spaces. Just imagine getting to know interesting folks disguised as yourself.

In the rich recesses of mind, you'll hunt for clues of all kinds. For pieces that fit, through mysterious puzzles you'll sift and you'll sort 'til understanding you'll get. You may change your perceptions as you solve and you stew. But, I promise, by the time your tale is through, you'll be wiser by far, knowing more than a few.

WHY THE *MOTHER MEMOIR?*

There is memoir and then there is the *Mother Memoir.*

*If you could tell just one small story that would capture
your mother's character and keep her spirit alive
into the future, what would it be?*

This is the seminal question I asked people over a decade ago after my mother died of Alzheimer's disease. I began what I now recognize as a spiritual journey inspiring women and men from all walks of life to write the *Mother Memoir.* I was filled with a burning desire to guide them to that tender spot deep inside themselves to locate striking memories and then to show them how they could turn even the hint of fragrance, the turn of a phrase, the hum of a tune, the flash of an eye, the back of a hand, or a fragment of family ritual, temporarily eclipsed in memory, into successful and unforgettable short, true tales. The *Mother Memoir* has the power to move people and change awareness.

An initial shift in my awareness actually summoned my pioneering effort into this place of treasure I call the *Mother Memoir.* In company with countless daughters and sons, I witnessed with great sadness, pain, and mounting disbelief the ravages of mental deterioration as my mother's ever creeping inability to recognize me became irrevocable. How could this be? I was with her 24/7 during her last three years, how could she not know me? A tragical shift, yes. A sharp-edged turn that took with it my being *known* by my mother while she lived, but also one that moved tragedy through inspiration to a source of satisfaction that would keep her spirit and hosts of spirits alive for years to come.

There inevitably comes a time when it is too late for each of us to ask mom how she would describe the spirit of her mother—always a tough lesson to learn. I knew my grandmother well, and I heard many a story about her from the town folk as I grew up in a small community in North Dakota, but I would love to know the one story my mother would have written as most telling about her mother's character and spirit. I feel a personal loss and regret because I no longer have the luxury to elicit stories from my mother about anyone who held a significant place in her heart, those who were connected to her soul. I hope you won't wait until it is too late to coax stories out of family members and to write your personal *Mother Memoir* so future generations reading your words will catch a glimpse of your mother's character and spirit.

The *Mother Memoir* is literary nonfiction, and you'll learn throughout this guidebook how to turn one memory of your mother into a remarkable story. You can also view the *Mother Memoir* as the basis or the point from which to begin writing memoir that may lead to longer works. Writing personal stories is an avenue to challenging myths, healing psychological wounds, soul-searching, and connecting to something larger than one's self. The beauty in the *TellTale Souls* method is that you will inadvertently realize your deepest self-truths in your quest to discover the underlying truths found by taking a close look at the character of the woman you will choose to play the major role in your story. I have been an eyewitness to the courage it takes for women and men to travel to and through their most memorable and intimate recollections and, with a little practice and soul-searching, to make the internal connections it takes to write with honesty.

It is accurate to say your being began with mom—she was your first relationship—she gave you life. Writing about her with honest emotion is the best place to start the memoir process; doing so will breathe new life into your conscious actions. When you stop to think about it, stories are all we have, and each of us has a particular story and a distinct voice. Similarly, various cultures, religions, and family traditions are rooted in stories spun as golden threads radiating from the core of the rich and multicolored human tapestry, a fabric binding us together as one and reminding us of what it means to be human. From woman comes life, from life…stories. From the *Mother Memoir*, the circle widens.

What is this single story you will tell about your mother, grandmother, or another woman from whom you felt a motherly connection? This isn't a question I want you to answer just yet; I simply want you to keep the thought of it uppermost in your mind, as each of you follows your particular path through this guidebook. Powerful images and unique insights will make themselves known to you when you consider deeply the memories that will be revealed as you look for the essence of your mother and illuminate her character through a true story, as no photograph could ever do.

It has been said a picture is worth a thousand words. I say a picture complements a thousand words, and that's why I like to add, whenever possible, the complement of a picture at the end of each published story. I recommend you do the same with the story you are about to write. Although bringing your mother's spirit to life or portraying her character in so short a space as a few pages is not altogether a simple feat, it has a more potent and honest effect than that of a mere photograph. Your words filled with the genuine emotion needed to capture mom's character in a short, true story will accomplish more than a two-dimensional photograph, which may have been staged to create a certain atmosphere or camaraderie that was not authentic.

Writing memoir is an act of honest creativity, just like tapping into memory can be thought of as brainstorming creatively, which is always fun, and I'll ask you to do this later on through interesting exercises. Creativity is used to provide answers to questions about why people significant in our lives acted as they did. The entire act and art of writing the *Mother Memoir* is nothing more or less than creative brainstorming, since answers are provided in an adventurous and out-of-the-box way. How can our memories be reduced to a conventional approach based on pure logic, when they are alive with emotion specifically felt in our own unique and subjective way?

In taking a new slant on the art and craft of writing memoir, it is my belief that your story will be of greatest personal consequence when your work is neither confined by convention nor measured by predetermined notions of what your story should be. You don't want to be limited and neither should your mother's spirit be cramped by rules. My angle of intent is to keep you from becoming bogged down by a system of order, the conventional way writing is taught, so that your natural creativity is not hampered, allowing you to discover more about yourself and your mother while chronicling her spirit. As you travel with me through this guidebook, arranged in five acts or stages to accomplishment, I welcome you to this invigorating vision as a partner in the tried-and-true *TellTale Souls* memoir writing method I've developed over the past decade.

The *Mother Memoir* is an opening to truth and understanding: truth that is met when you take the time to greet and revisit memories with an openness of mind and understanding that will ripen through your time spent musing and writing. The art of capturing character is not about tracing the life history of your mother; rather it is about writing a vignette revealing the essence of her spirit by expressing the effect of a particular incident or event, an anecdote, or combined moments in time that will reveal who she is at her core. And it's through telltale stories,

5

bio-vignettes that compel awareness, appreciation, and unity, that we find the ultimate connections.

> **WRITE**: List ten reasons why you think discovering what makes your mother tick and writing about her as an individual would be easy or difficult, painful or pleasurable.

TELL TALE SOULS METHOD

The *TellTale Souls* method is an imaginative process of discovery and connection rather than an academic sort of discipline.

Through Five Acts to accomplishment, memoir writing is demystified for writers of any level as they learn techniques to access memory and create true and telling tales with a thoughtful openness of mind and the intent to look closely at someone other than themselves.

Memories, perceptions, feelings, and emotions are processed through reflection, *innersearch*, and stimulating creative writing exercises. A powerful focus on voice, truth, honesty, alternative ways of thinking and being, and new understanding gives rise to a universal linking of our spirits.

BIO-VIGNETTE

Why bio-vignette? "Bio" signifies a story written essentially about someone other than yourself, and "vignette" is a small grouping of movements, moments, notes, actions, or events that in the case of *Mother Memoir* are pulled together into a literary sketch capturing character. Bio-vignette is comfortable and appropriate; it fits what we're going to achieve.

Throughout this book, I use the terms vignette, bio-vignette, memoir, telling tale, and story interchangeably. The bio-vignettes I suggest are generally between two to five pages in length or around 800 to 1,600 words.

TellTale Soul's succinct definition of bio-vignette: Your short, descriptive story capturing the character and spirit of someone who had a significant, motherly impact on your life.

Throughout the story you are here to write, you will focus energy toward paying tribute to or better understanding someone other than yourself; consequently, when all is said and done, the result will be a deeper understanding of yourself after exploring that relationship. Writing an autobiographical memoir, where you are the primary subject of the story, has a markedly different effect than writing the *Mother Memoir*. When the focus is on you, the autobiographer, the urge to self-protect tends to shroud you in subjective secrecy so that your innermost thoughts and feelings will not be so openly displayed; moreover, disappointment stemming from unpleasant incidents and fault are often projected on to someone else. Writing a bio-vignette has a refreshingly opposite effect.

WRITE three paragraphs about an incident where you believe you were wronged in some way by anyone—a parent, friend, or coworker, perhaps a physician or politician. Let your feelings flow, rip the offending party apart on paper, cast stones, cuss if you must, feel justified in your anger.

Only after you have completed the step above, and you feel justified in your response, write a few paragraphs standing in the presumably offending party's shoes to check out the other side of the story. This exercise is a must to orient you toward writing with greater objectivity while seeking truth in relationships.

Unless your purpose for writing memoir is for personal revenge or exposé, the desire to write memoir stems from a sincere need to know, to learn, to understand, as well as a willingness to examine your present perceptions of intimate family relationships. The act of reflecting on the character of someone other than yourself in a memoir deserves high praise. Emphasis on self is given too high a priority today. Granted, you play a big part in your *Mother Memoir*, but you narrow the gap between yourself and understanding mom when you direct energy toward telling the truth and looking at her in her own right—as an individual—when you write a deceptively simple story.

Since the word "deceptive" could imply that your story is misleading or untrue, don't let that throw you off track. It's not the stories themselves that are deceptive; it's the idea that a memoir, a bio-vignette of say 800-1600 words, may not be long enough to get your point across or be impactful. Longer is better? Not so. By following the *TellTale Souls* method, where the essential impact of immediacy and intimacy are implicit, your story will fully illuminate the significance of your mother's character and spirit. You will become a more focused, energized writer.

Those exceptional souls—both women and men—who preceded you in writing their bio-vignettes, found that it was one of the most meaningful, fulfilling accomplishments they had ever achieved. It is fair to say this statement rings true for all of the *TellTale Souls* who have embarked on this stimulating adventure and reached the other side more thoughtful, more knowing, and more satisfied—far richer for the experience.

> **WRITE** for ten minutes on why you believe it is important for you to write a bio-vignette about your mother—for this exercise do write about your mother, rather than someone else.

WHO IS A *TELLTALE SOUL*?

Simple answer: A writer of the
Mother Memoir.

TellTale Souls are people who have the courage to look deeply into personal memories and then to shape certain striking ideas into short, true stories. The resulting bio-vignettes will satisfy their individual needs to better understand, honor, and allow the spirit of their mothers to live on in the hearts and minds of family and friends.

The threads *TellTale Souls* spin resonate universally on multiple levels. The hearts of strangers are also touched, because it is in truths shared through story that we connect intuitively to the essence of primal female wisdom. Reading the *Mother Memoirs* inspires others to write and to share telling tales.

While reading the story examples throughout this book, you'll find a stronger connection to some than to others. By *listening with care* to each ordinary woman's authentic voice, as she weaves a lasting impression of her mother, you will gain insight into what it means to be a *TellTale Soul.*

One woman, after her first *TellTale Soul* class, commented, *"I know I slept last night, but I kept waking up and thinking and remembering. I just want you to know what a profoundly meaningful experience working with you was for me. In order to move forward those many years ago and get on with my life, I slammed a lot of doors....I suspect that behind those doors, some of which are still closed, lurk many memories I'm still not in touch with. Knowing that there are ALL these women willing to talk about their mothers, both in glowing and painful terms, gave me permission, as well as a frame of reference, to think about and interpret many of the things I've not really revisited....a HUGE thank you, Lynn, for getting me started down this path."*

One man, after completing his *Mother Memoir*, said, *"I went through a whole gamut of emotions writing this story, reliving all those previously dormant memories of frustration and restrained lifestyle while growing up. Yet, all the while, feeling this powerful love—the lifeline thread that held my brothers and me together with our mother. This journey, this experience, has been one that I would highly recommend."*

As you begin, I believe it is helpful to set a goal so that you have a clear idea of what you are striving for. Within that goal you will find both quantitative aspects and qualitative rewards. The first part of your goal is to write just one story, a bio-vignette, capturing the character or essence of your mother, one which you will record for posterity. The second part of your goal, the narrative aspect, brings to light and pays tribute to the universality of the soul.

The stories are about synergy and communion where truth lies in the stories of ordinary people's lives and reveals the inner workings of their souls as myriad possibilities for embracing life unfold. You will discover that a certain memory or an unpretentious *slice of life* will take on a tangible meaning of its own as you capture it on paper. Using this book as your guide, you will find effective ways and ample opportunity to bring memories into focus. Focusing on powerful memories will give you time to reflect upon them without distraction and help you find the best way to preserve them with clarity.

When memories do float in, please allow yourself the time and space to contemplate their significance. Whether they are memories that you cherish and reveling in them is sweet, even poignantly so, or whether particular dark memories fill your being and call for a bolstering of inner strength so that you can begin to understand them, this is the time to consciously connect to the soul-line. This is your opportunity, in the present time, to gain greater self-realization and universal understanding by paying tribute to and acknowledging the wonders inherent in the soul of humanity.

So much is being said about the healing qualities of writing, journaling, or keeping a diary. These avenues to healing are powerful. Through my experience helping people write stories that chiefly reveal someone other than themselves, I've witnessed a leap to an even higher level of healing. Awareness takes a wider stance when we give someone other than ourselves center stage in a story. Through memories that impact us like no other, we hunger for the truths we find in the actions of other people. In writing down what we have found, we find comfort. At a talk given several years ago at Dominican University by Jean Shinoda Bolen, M.D., after she published *Close to the Bone,* one single sentence has stayed with me always: *"We are spiritual beings on a human path and sometimes we need a story more than we need food."* Wise words we can take to heart from a Jungian analyst and prolific, celebrated author.

Marie, a *TellTale Soul,* told me that she studied and earned a degree in psychology and went through therapy where she tried to forgive and made excuses for her mother's behavior. She went on to say, *"Telling this story was a good experience for me, and I've since done much soul searching and writing, exploring the negative experiences in the relationship between my mother and myself. I now realize that the pain around my relationship with her is gone. What I'm left with today is called health!"*

A young man said, *"Thank you for the occasion to explore and better understand the significance of women and make peace with personal issues. I see my mother in a whole new way after this difficult but rewarding experience of writing about her. Taking a new look at long buried issues, through more grown up eyes, I began to realize some things were not as I had thought they were for so many years. I asked for her forgiveness and she gave it to me."*

Interestingly, another woman, who participated in a memoir writing class I led, was fully prepared to write a bio-vignette about her paternal grandmother; in fact, she did write a touching story about her grandmother. On the first evening, however, she announced that she had no intention of writing about her mother—that subject was way too complicated, and she did not want to write anything uncomplimentary about this woman whom she loved, but who had also caused her considerable pain. By week two, however, she had switched gears and began a story about her mother which she subsequently completed and then gave to her mother as a gift on Mother's Day. That took strength and courage.

By now I think you realize, in the overall picture, there is an unspecified outcome directed toward you in this process of writing a bio-vignette about your mother. One immediate advantage is that if the story you will write is the first story you have ever written, you now can move forward to write all you have ever dreamed of writing, whether that be nonfiction or fiction, since you will then trust that you have the voice and creative talent to write. For those who are adept at writing, after completing your journey here, you may look at writing through a different lens—one that focuses on the power generated by the art and craft of writing your *Mother Memoir.*

CONSIDERING THE *MOTHER MEMOIR* A GIFT

I have often used "Give the Gift of Story" as the title for workshops and presentations. Although that phrase now sounds a little dated to me, that simple idea will always be appreciated and valued. I see the idea of giving and receiving gifts of memoir from several angles. However, not everyone sees the gift angle as I do, partly due to the fact that their mothers may no longer be here to accept a gift or that the painful memories included in their *Mother Memoir* do not seem a suitable gift. But gifts are not always two-sided—one side realized by the giver, the other side acknowledged by the recipient—although this is often the goal in gift giving. Consummating both sides is not necessary for a satisfying outcome.

As you write a heartwarming, even poignant, memoir, it is a natural to want to give it as a gift to the person you have chosen to portray. You believe your gesture will be well received, and you can imagine, for example, your grandmother's delight in reading it—a memoir where you've taken the time to look at her as an individual. What's more, your gift of memoir will preserve treasured memories of her spirit, as well as your relationship with her for years to come.

On the other hand, some of you may turn away from thinking about your memoir as a gift because the person you pick as your main character and the experience you intend to use as the basis for your story are unpleasant, or worse. Obviously, in this situation and from your point of view, you certainly don't think of this particular memoir as a gift. However, from my point of view, it is truly a gift. If you don't deem it appropriate as a gift to give her, then accept it as a gift you will give to yourself through the act of writing it and learning from it.

For those of you whose stories about "mothers" bring up dreadful, heartwrenching memories, you will write through painful experiences, and you will come to some understanding about what happened due to the fact that you have opened your mind to those things buried deep inside and placed the painful events out in the open through the process of writing memoir. You might decide not to let anyone else ever read what you've written. That's okay. The story can be for your eyes only. When you make this process fully intentional and take personal control over the emotions linked to the events, you have given yourself a very special gift. It could just be the best gift you will ever receive.

WRITE two pages detailing your reasons why you think writing *Mother Memoir* will be a gift. A gift to whom? You as the writer, or the woman the story is about? And why is this so? Concentrate, locate your precise feelings and thoughts and expand on them. Just to say, "It would make Mom happy," or "I believe it will help me heal some of the wounds from my past," is not enough. Get down to the nitty-gritty. What changes could this act of writing bring about in you, in her? Why will it bring up anger or joy, for example, and how do you perceive it will be manifest? Above all, be completely honest with yourself. No one else will read this, unless you want them to.

Any way you look at it, *Mother Memoir* is the most powerful of gifts. How many times have you been at your wit's end after asking the women, especially the older ones, in your family to give you even a hint of what they might like for their birthdays, Christmas, and other special days? You would love to give them something they really want, but their answers to your question often sound a lot like this: "I don't need a thing, honey, but, if you feel you must, I could use some nice hand lotion. I do like chocolates, but I shouldn't—mostly I'd like to see you." Can you imagine how much you would please them by the gift of your *Mother Memoir*? Yes, I know that will simply not work for some of you, and I think you know what I am going to say—write that story as a gift to yourself.

For those of you who plan to give your story to the woman about whom you have written, there are many ways to package your gift. You will probably come up with several of your own inventive and imaginative ways, but here are a few from me:

> ➤ For that perfect personal touch, consider writing your story in your finest longhand—cursive—or print it, if you never learned cursive. A little aside here: I learned a couple of years ago, much to my astonishment, that one of my daughters, a Phi Beta Kappa in finance from a top university, was never taught to write in cursive—she prints beautifully and is a whiz at texting, so it doesn't bother her in the least, and I know I would love a story from her any way she wanted to deliver it to me, but I hope she doesn't text it, my screen is awfully small!

> ➤ If you are skilled at calligraphy, this art form would be a lovely way to present your gift of story. According to the wisegeek.com, "Calligraphy is the art of writing script in such a way as to express the beauty of what is being written in the formation of the letters themselves."

➤ So many people now seem to have a penchant for the keyboard—this works, too, and you can experiment with different fonts, embed photos into your document, and have some fun with special characters to make it more personal. Of course you can even attach it to an email, although delivering it in person would offer the greatest impact; remember she would like to spend time with you.

➤ Complementing your telling tale with a photograph or several of them will provide additional flavor. Get ready for tears and laughter.

➤ If you are delivering your gift in person, which by all means do so, be sure to take along writing supplies. This is an ideal time to elicit stories from her. In fact, wrap up those writing supplies with a copy of *TellTale Souls Writing the Mother Memoir* to encourage her to write stories on her own before it is too late.

Finally, consider the gifting opportunities your family tree affords. Laying gifts of story upon those branches will add immeasurable dimension. Most of us have a skeletal diagram of our lineage where the names and dates of our ancestors and the newly arrived are recorded on the branches of our family tree. But the character of these important people, especially our female ancestors, since the woman's role in the family and society has historically been taken for granted, first becomes blurred and then ultimately lost. The very *stuff* of life itself has been left out—there is no color, depth, emotion, no character in the diagram of a family tree no matter how artfully it is designed. Illuminating the character of your mother through your gift of story will allow you to begin to fill out your family tree in a meaningful way. The first blushes of bud are shimmering on my family tree with the stories my sister and I wrote honoring our relationship with Mother after her death and with the stories my daughters have written about me.

If you don't write it down, it will be lost.
Wouldn't that be a shame?

There is nothing like remembering or paying tribute to a person who holds a significant place in our lives with a simple and honest written record. And there is nothing like the power of writing to cleanse the soul and provide a deeper understanding of people and events that hold significance in our lives. It is worth mentioning, again, that a photograph captures only a look at best, whereas a bio-vignette captures aspects of character and spirit set with more complexity. The men and women I have encountered, since beginning my teaching, have thoughtfully written stories illuminating the character of at least one person they value. In so doing, the memories they have preserved added dimension to the previously bare branches on their family trees. It's your turn now.

DEMYSTIFYING MEMORY

What is memory anyway? I love how Aristotle pithily described it, "Memory is the scribe of the soul." Is memory something that keeps us anchored to the past for better or for worse? Do you perceive it as a place you would rather not go, because you find past experiences produce anxiety that you don't want to wrestle with? Or is a trip down memory lane a great joy whereby you allow yourself to spend time simply luxuriating? Perhaps you want to get in touch with memories that have heretofore evaded your conscious thoughts. You will explore these ideas through the prompts and memory exercises in Act Two.

The power of memory is no secret, but the mystery that surrounds memory is very real. Memory is the echo of your mind. Memory is a reference, a record, and guide. It is made up of impressions set in your brain's neural pathways that can be accessed readily or maddeningly elusive. You sometimes ask yourself why you cannot remember the details of certain events when other memories are crystal clear. It can be that you are not being mindful—not really focusing—or you are unwilling to accept the images or thoughts you have created in your mind at a certain point in time. You may recall them later. Take to heart another wise quote from Aristotle, "It often happens that, though a person cannot recollect at the moment, yet by seeking he can do so, and discovers what he seeks."

In writing memoir, we strive to bring back and fully realize the people, places, things, actions, emotions, concepts, and even indefinable impressions captured through any and all sensory means, which we previously squirreled away in memory, as witness to our lives. We use sight, hearing, taste, touch, and smell with a pinch of imagination to recall what was. You will begin to recognize memory by fleeting images, which at first you can't quite contain if they were held deep within you, and as ephemeral feelings struggling to emerge into the daylight of your mind. By greeting those fleeting images and ephemeral feelings you give them credence and yourself a belief that what you are looking for is there, within your reach.

WRITE one page listing events, interactions, or situations pertaining to your relationship with your mother that you want to remember with more clarity. While making the list, note any details or ideas that come to mind, even if they don't make sense at the time. Save this list for later reference in our work together.

It is interesting to consider the idea that memory is not really there, it is not present, until we acknowledge or identify it by bringing it into consciousness through memory exercises or it simply pops up spontaneously as we go about our daily lives or nightly treks. Take a look at an individual diagnosed with amnesia, who is said to have lost his memory. Yet later, through time or a jarring event, he regains his memory. Was what was lost found? Was it ever gone? Mysterious memory it is.

Of one thing I am sure, memory is both a dynamic and an intoxicating force that is a living, breathing integral part of our personal makeup. Based on memory, we chart courses of action and accept or deny ideas and the people fixed in them. Memory is not static; it takes on the characteristics of a chameleon, changing color through time and tone. It intoxicates with a flare as it drives us to dig deep into memories to revel in our successes, to rehash difficult or dangerous times, and to relive exciting times. Writing *Mother Memoir* is nothing if not stimulating and all on the account of memory.

After recalling compelling, intoxicating memories, remember you have the upper hand. It is within your power to make sense of what you remember. Memory may be dynamic, but it need not control you. Moving memory to memoir is a time for things to flow out of you onto paper through truth and with an honest intent and desire to better understand significant past experiences.

Lynn Cook Henriksen

GETTING IN TOUCH WITH MEMORIES

You have a memory bank seething with possibilities—
possibilities waiting for your exploration and respect. Have
no doubt, you will find the memory that will be the stimulus for
the story you will write characterizing that certain someone. But
you must first observe what is going on before you put it down
on paper. Make your process intentional.

It could be you have tucked away memories so securely in
your subconscious that it will take some probing and prodding
to awaken them, but quite possibly all it will take is for you to
sink into a quiet place so that they can surface. Look at this as
finding an opening through which you will peer into the hidden
folds of your mind and find a memory that propels you to move
forward and turn what you have recalled into a memoir.

On the other hand, some of you may be forever going back
to certain memories from long ago that just won't let you be.
Frequently occurring and persistent memories present
themselves to all of us from time to time. Authors have written
entire books based on one memory they could not let go.
Writing your *Mother Memoir* may revolve around one of your
persistent memories about your mom. A poignant story, written
by Karen, a *TellTale Soul*, centers around the "look" she gave her
mother years ago. This powerful memory haunted her as she
thought about it over and over again throughout the years. She
said writing her bio-vignette, giving that certain recurrent
memory over to paper, and finally presenting it to her mother set

22

her free. I have seen her shed tears in group settings when I have asked her to read her story aloud.

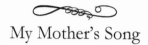

My Mother's Song
~Karen Welch-Coleman

My mother has always been my protector, my ally, and my soul mate. I was safe in her care, protected from cruelty and derision. She is my sanctuary, my safe place. I have always had the knowledge that through her I am loved, no matter what. She gave me the strength to survive the hard experiences that would be part of my life. My greatest regret is that I deprived her of the same pure love in a moment of pure selfishness.

During a church service we were standing, singing a hymn. It was a powerful hymn that inspired the singers to sing at fortissimo, with spirit. As I stood in front of my mother, hearing her beautiful soprano voice singing in praise, I decided she was singing too loudly. Why I decided that or upon what I based my decision I'll never know. It could only have been an adolescent attitude of not being "cool." I judged her as singing too loudly. I turned around and gave her what must have been and what has come to be called "the look."

In that moment, I learned the absolute meaning of power, and of the power I truly possessed. The look on my mother's face was one of true pain and hurt. I discovered the power to destroy another human being, her joy in simple pleasures, her joy in life. The moment when my mother ceased to sing was the most frightening of my life. She closed her hymnal and stood silent. Absolutely silent. By the end of the verse, I hated what I had done. I opened a hymnal and turned to hand it to her. Her eyes, the color of a vibrant blue summer sky, always warm with love, were now ice blue, the pain startlingly visible. Being the kind person she is, she took the hymnal from me, but she didn't resume singing. I don't think there was any way at that place in time that she could have found her voice. It had been silenced by her oldest daughter's cruelty. The pain was too great. I had embarrassed my mother as only her child could.

The blessing of my childhood and my life is that my mother is a spiritual, loving, caring, and compassionate person. She teaches through example, the way she lives her life. Random acts of kindness were a part of my mother's life long before they became chic. Forgiveness is always granted, never withheld.

It was perhaps not that exact day in chapel that I chose to turn away from that dark side of my spirit. But it was the clarifying event that solidified the path I would attempt to follow—and the person's life I would try to emulate.

I vowed not to silence anyone's joy ever again. Instead, I would work to follow Mother's example by recognizing and reinforcing the talents and abilities of others. I would strive to be compassionate, looking for ways to communicate soul-to-soul and attending to the needs of others.

My mother will probably leave this life before I do, and I know I will feel again the pain I inflicted upon her 35 years ago—the emptiness, the sorrow, the momentary lapse in her joy of song and life. But when I pass from this mortal existence, I hope the first sound I hear will be my mother's beautiful soprano voice singing my welcome.

Photo contributed by Karen: In the rose garden with Mother.

Karen Welch-Coleman: "As the oldest of eight children, I have always had a very close and symbiotic relationship with my mother. She has nurtured, cherished, and forgiven me when needed. One of my deepest regrets was a careless and cruel moment during my teenage years that she in no way deserved. I've wanted to take that moment back more often than I can count over my life's journey. May the sharing of this experience pay tribute to her and provide redemption for me."

Like Karen, do persistent memories pester you for a reason? Plague you nonstop? Pluck at your heartstrings? Do you whisk them away like pests because they make your heart beat faster, bring a smile up from deep inside that you won't take the time to savor, or do you fear remembering times you'd rather forget? Maybe you actually think you are too busy to honor, respect, or try to understand the importance of your past by revisiting your memories.

Take the time to discover what these persistent memories are there to tell you—they are vying for your attention. But do it with a purpose. History does repeat itself, if only in memory. Memories are brimming with intention. Ask yourself, "If not now, then when will I do justice to my memories?" Begin your journey by looking a memory or two full in the face. Then pick just one compelling memory and write your bio-vignette.

What will fall into place when you write memoir? Only you can answer that question, and the best way to do it is by looking at each recurring memory carefully and setting pen to paper. There is much to discover by paying attention to what you find deep inside. You will find that your new role as a memory sleuth may free you to live a life more fully yours.

As you go through this book and work with the exercises and activities that follow, keep a pad of paper and pencil at the ready to jot down words, phrases, or impressions that you find interesting or speak to you intimately. Do this as they emerge—images are fleeting.

As I'm sure many of you have experienced, moments of inspiration are ignited when you read stories written by others. This happens because you identify with something the author wrote; the way one of the characters acts or looks in your mind's eye; the colloquialisms apparent in dialogue; or part of a scene, location, or setting is described in such a way that you are instantly transported there.

You never know when inspiration will hit. As you go throughout your day, keep sticky notes close at hand:

- ➤ on the nightstand
- ➤ on the desk
- ➤ in the car
- ➤ near the telephone
- ➤ next to the kitchen sink
- ➤ on the gardening bench
- ➤ yes, even in the bathroom, where some of the best material and ideas arise

---

WRITE two long paragraphs about the impact of recurrent memories. In the first paragraph write your reaction to Karen's story above, "My Mother's Song." Make the second paragraph personal, write about a recurrent memory of your mother that visits you often and the effect it has on you.

FINDING INSPIRATION

The seeds of inspiration are sown by ordinary writers of the *Mother Memoir* and reaped by readers, who relish the connections found in small flashes of detail and description through which they find connection. I wrote the following story, "The French Lesson," about my best friend's mother, who was like a second mother to me in many respects while growing up. As you read the story take note of words, phrases, depictions of character and setting, and anything else that stands out for you. If something you read rings a memory bell or hits a nerve, take that as a sign you have a similar personal memory itching to get out.

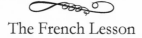

The French Lesson

~Lynn Henriksen

The "stocking seam" up the back of her leg drawn on in pencil before mass, if she'd run out of hosiery. A broad, self-conscious smile, when she received a compliment, revealed her pleasure at having been appreciated. Her cheeks looked happy. A tight, sturdy little body standing proud even with the bent end of a bobby pin probing her ear—they perpetually itched, and evidently my mother hadn't ever told her, "You never put anything smaller than your elbow in your ear." Anyway, her husband often had one of those long chain-link type key chains wrapped around one of his ears, so they made a good pair. A profusion of touching images I cannot contain float through my mind at the thought of Leona, Lee for short. She was my best friend's mother, whom I claim as my second mother and love dearly.

She had a great laugh, which she often tried to conceal when something amused her but didn't want to give herself away—like when Colette and I tried to get away with bending the rules a bit. She'd have to reel back in the laugh that had impulsively escaped and attempt to look stern. Then she'd manage a flimsy, "Oh, you girls," and we'd know we were off the hook. From childhood on, Colette and I were inseparable, spending great chunks of time in prolonged overnights in each other's homes. Lee treated me like one of her daughters; as an "insider," I knew her.

The most indelible and poignant memory I have of Lee is better understood with a backdrop of the 1940s and '50s. Father Knows Best looks smarmy to us now, but in the scheme of things, it wasn't that long ago that television shows like that were a standard to live up to. If a woman was a "good" wife and mother, the pride she took in washing, ironing, cooking, cleaning, and supporting hubby while raising the children single handedly (with an occasional night out for bridge or dinner) should have been fulfilling enough. If it wasn't, she didn't complain. If she did complain, Valium would have been suggested. Lee was a classic woman of those times, raising three daughters and catering to a husband who loved her but was blind to the possibilities neglected in and omitted from her life.

The clear, distinct sound of a well modulated, sexy male voice drifted through the screened-in summer porch where Colette and I lay stomached on the cool linoleum playing gin rummy. His presence may not have so immediately grabbed our attention if the language he was speaking hadn't been French. We'd heard just enough French phrases tossed about here and there to identify the language, but this was not something we were used to hearing in the backyards of our small, North Dakota town. We looked up from our game, locking eyes with the simultaneous, unspoken question, "Who's that?" Then a voice that sounded suspiciously like Lee's voice responded to this Frenchman . . . in French! What was going on here? The two of us dropped our cards and slide-crawled, elbows and thighs to stay low, over to the edge of the screen door so that we could sneak a look out in the direction of the mysterious voices.

Seated beside a phonograph perched on a tray table, electrical cord draped across the grass, up the side of the house and through the window was Lee, grammar book in hand. She was intently studying the foreign words and hesitantly parroted them back to her Frenchman when he paused and spun lazily on a black, grooved 78. I suppose Colette and I were hoping for something more clandestine.

That scene has remained so palpably fresh in my mind that I can feel the weight of the thick August air, smell the dusty grass, and hear the leaves rustle softly in the big tree that served as canopy from the sun while Lee studied. We watched her silently for some time, drawn into her world. But we knew we wouldn't be welcome there. Somehow we sensed the intimacy and urgency that so enmeshed her in that lesson in French. She had French Canadian blood in her veins, and she craved something beyond those things that the everyday brought her.

Lee had a hand in raising my self-esteem throughout the years. She liked me for a lot of reasons and told me what they were. The impact of even her innocuous, off-hand comments have stayed with me for a lifetime. But my most potent memory of her is when she unknowingly revealed to me that a woman has needs just for herself—that was the lesson I learned the afternoon of the French lesson.

Photo contributed by Lynn: Kissing Lee's foxy cheek.

Lynn Henriksen: "It gave me great pleasure to write this bio-vignette framing the delightful woman who is my best friend's mother. She doled out wisdom by the way she lived her life—there were seldom any sermons."

Close your eyes—pause and consider the details of the story. Now ask yourself these important questions:

- ➤ What is really happening here?
- ➤ How do I feel about this story?
- ➤ What picture came to mind about this mother?
- ➤ Which words, phrases, and images stood out?
- ➤ What caught my attention?
- ➤ What made me smile? Tear up?
- ➤ What made me remember?
- ➤ How did this woman come alive for me?
- ➤ What sense do I have of this woman and why?
- ➤ Did I find a common bond?
- ➤ Could that voice have been mine?
- ➤ Did this mother remind me of anyone?

MAKE NOTES: Use the story of "The French Lesson" while considering each of the questions above. Go back through the story to thoroughly answer each question.

This list can be invaluable to you. Make it a critical part of your journey. Use it again and again when you mindfully read other stories *and* while writing your bio-vignette.

PLANNING BEFORE YOU ACT

Please do some planning before you start writing your story. As they say, "Don't put the cart before the horse." You won't get where you want to go without thinking ahead. As you leave Act One and begin to get down to the business of actually writing your story some practical advice up front will get you going down the right track.

If you think you write a story from the first sentence to the last, that it just tumbles out of you with perfect precision and form, you probably won't even get started.

Your story will evolve—this is one of the most important points for you to remember as you begin your *Mother Memoir.* Writing this bio-vignette means starting with a memory of interest to use as your focal point, the theme of your memoir. You will develop this theme by molding your ideas into a story and bringing your characters to life through various techniques that we will explore throughout this book. It is a process, but it is not linear—that would not be nearly as much fun!

As a typical writer, you will move forward and backward and around again through your story many times and write several drafts, although for our purposes here, this does not require a long and arduous journey.

The author, Cesare Pavese, said, "We do not remember days; we remember moments." In Act Two you will find many interesting exercises to help you tap into moments in time and to seize upon a compelling incident or event that you'll use as the core or theme of your short, true tale. Then you will begin by writing an entire version early on so that you have the bones of your memoir set out before you. By doing this, you will realize that you can, indeed, write this important story, and you'll have set your story in motion with the parts at hand to mold at your will.

Think about the sculptors who say the statue is inside the block of marble. Their only task is to shape it and refine it so that the work of art can emerge. Michelangelo said, "Every block of stone has a statue inside it and it is the task of the sculptor to discover it." He also said, "I saw the angel in the marble and carved until I set him free." I do not imagine all of you will find an angel in your story, but many of you will. For those who have not such a pretty story to tell, exchange the word angel for devil and you will still get your first version out of the quarry.

The purpose of the *TellTale Souls* method is to encourage spontaneity and focus on writing short memoir. There is really no need for elaborate timelines or theoretical writing models in the work you are doing here, where you will be writing about specific moments in time and capturing the character and spirit of your mother, around which your story revolves. If you come to a point, after completing your bio-vignette, where you plan to turn your work into a full-length memoir or a piece of fiction, you will have a very good start.

Now get comfortable with the medium you plan to use to write your memoir. If you use a word processor to write, it will make your life considerably easier when you want to move things around, make additions, or edit your story.

On to other mediums to capture stories—paper, that wonderful, dare I say, nostalgic stuff of many colors, weights, and sizes, loose leaf or bound, is still the choice of many writers. And let's not forget the smell of the perfectly sharpened lead pencil (You know, the one that made that ugly bump form on the middle finger of your writing hand in third grade.) and the way it glided smoothly over your paper in penmanship class while making loops and lines just so. But the black smudges left on the page from a badly worn-down eraser or the tearing of your paper when the metal band got its way, still won't be welcomed. And then there are those who can't write a word unless they hold their favorite pen in hand—the trusty ball point or the fluid fountain. Whatever pleases you—use it, because that is what will work for you.

A note about handwriting and plain old, precious paper: Perhaps one of the most poignant things we come across are old letters, notes, scribbles in margins of books, or captions on photographs written in the hand of someone who passed before us. Nothing can be finer than to run across handwriting on vintage paper. It is innately sensual. We recognize people by a certain flourish of their pen or their far left- or right-lilting patterns scrolling across the page. We watch young people grow up as they refine their penmanship, make it part of their personalities. On the other hand, we have all noticed the physical or mental decline apparent in the shakier hand-strokes of the infirm and the aged.

Most of us cherish those first scrawlings of our babies, letters connecting loved ones, and even the shortest of handwritten notes. For over half a century, I have kept the tiniest piece of worn paper in my dad's unique handwriting that simply says *Little Bug*, his pet name for me. And when I take down the old *Joy of Cooking* and see the notes my mother made remarking on certain recipes or changing many of them to suit her taste, I find it difficult to fully express how reading her handwriting speaks to my soul on many secret levels, complete with layers of emotions and the triggering of a gamut of memories.

Many believe you can read the character of people by their handwriting alone. I think about the bittersweet reminders of spirit we get when we see familiar handwriting, and I'm reminded that technology, notably email and texting, is well on its way to marking the end of those indelible marks and the pleasure we receive from personal handwritten messages.

Think about keeping a draft of your memoir written in your hand. Future generations will value your handwriting to be sure. And when your mother plays a hand at *Keeping Spirits Alive* through written reflections on *her mother*, let her know you would appreciate a copy in her handwriting.

Some people enjoy using a tape recorder or camcorder to add yet another dimension while crystallizing moments and recording the character of people significant in their lives. Both mediums are valuable, but these last two forms of communication should be used in conjunction with the written word, not as a replacement.

WRITE a letter, a real, honest to goodness letter to your mother—you can write this letter even if your mother has died or is incommunicado. A letter on paper in your handwriting will be meaningful, even if you are the only one who ever sees it, or it can be a keepsake, no matter who eventually reads it. Now don't just sign a birthday card—take the time to leave a lasting impression.

SETTING THE STAGE TO WRITE

The place you set up for yourself to write is strictly a personal choice. The space you need so that your creative juices can flow and the setting where you will feel most comfortable telling your story may be:

- ➢ a library
- ➢ the den
- ➢ your office
- ➢ a corner of your bedroom
- ➢ the community park
- ➢ a mountain retreat
- ➢ the hayloft
- ➢ the kitchen table
- ➢ a room with a view
- ➢ a coffee house

Make notes on each of these settings as to whether or not they are locations that may potentially work for you. Doing so will get your imagination in the mix thinking of places to write that may never have previously occurred to you.

The highly talented, bestselling author of *The House of Spirits* and many other novels and memoirs, Isabel Allende, confessed she goes into a windowless closet, often with only a candle, each January to begin her next novel or memoir. What will work for you? For some people a writing partner offers the stimulus needed to get started, as well as being an ongoing energizing force to stay positively charged. Discovering and applying various writing techniques, giving and receiving feedback, and sharing stories and insight are invaluable tools by which writers thrive and continue to grow.

You will want to establish a particular place to write on your own time no matter what. Which props will help you focus and get in the mood to write? Maybe all you require is a writing tablet and pencil or your fingers grazing the keyboard, while others need the comfort and inspiration that come from familiar things like candles, photographs, flowers, and music, or perhaps it is fresh air and the sounds of nature that provide the best results for you.

While I was working on my writing method and story collection, it was important to me to be surrounded by family pictures—especially those of Mom—and a growing assemblage of photographs complementing the stories sent to me by *TellTale Souls*. They continue to warm my heart as they provide welcomed inspiration. Looking at them confirms my deep-seated belief that a bio-vignette is a must in order to capture the character, left unsung in photos, of our mothers and to keep their spirits vibrant in the present and for future generations to better recognize their ancestors.

One day while musing about how to design the cover for my book, a picture on a shelf near my desk of Mom, looking pensively into the ocean from the deck of a steamship heading for Alaska, beckoned me. And that was that. The front cover would be designed around that simple photo my father had taken of her many years ago. Much to my amazement, rifling through more pictures strewn in an old cigar box, I discovered another picture of Mom on that same ship, but this picture depicted a different angle. Dad caught her from the back, in silhouette, as she leaned on the ship's handrail and contemplated the majesty of her view. I've placed this photo in the back of this book as the perfect ending. Apparently, an effective setting leads to affective expansion—the items with which you surround yourself while you write will influence your work.

Your work will also be affected by your energy level no matter the writing environment you have designed and designated as your own. It is essential to pick a time to write when you are most alert and distractions can be held to a minimum so those all important creative juices will flow freely. Then schedule a block of this time in your daily or weekly routine that is set aside strictly for writing. Make a standing appointment with yourself, your memories, and your writing.

Keeping the reason why you want to write memoir uppermost in your mind, **WRITE out a detailed plan** for when and where you will write and the length of time you will devote to it. Spend at least thirty minutes designing this all important plan. Do not make vague statements—I will try to write each morning before work—be specific in writing this agenda. You will succeed in your plan when you use declarative terminology and by making a practical, personally achievable plan. For example, "I will write on my laptop computer from 9 to 11 p.m. every Monday, Wednesday, and Saturday in the cozy alcove of my living room surrounded by the music that sets me in the mood for writing my memoir." This example is to the point, but you will make your plan personal by filling in complex descriptions of where and when you will write. You will add supplemental elements to enhance the time spent writing in your newly created space, making it a

home of comfort and the place to achieve
success.

The most important aspect of writing memoir is all about
interlacing place of mind and peace of mind. If you don't have
the ideal space in which to write, you can create the perfect place
in your mind and transport yourself there. Some people have the
luxury of spending time at writers' retreats, while others have
attained equal success without all those trappings by shutting out
the outside world and making peace within themselves by
keeping the promises they have made. So, don't spend time
bringing the outside world in when what is essential depends
upon your ability to bring the inside world out.

Act Two

A second act can be thought of as a place to reconsider our lives and relationships, shake up ideas, and question strongly held beliefs that have, thus far, directed our lives. By looking at our memories critically, all the while seeking truth, we have the chance to, shall we say, "Play it again, Sam."

And as far as stage plays go, act two can take up half the span or energy of a play. And I feel, in the overall scheme of writing bio-vignettes, this holds true here, too. Finding and making sense of your memories will take up fifty percent of your energy, and with the tension created by your findings you will write your heart out and produce a successfully written Mother Memoir.

AWAKENING MEMORIES

We are going to explore ways to stir up memories—
memories that will be at the heart of our rich tales
characterizing the spirits of our mothers. As we peer into the
subconscious, all kinds of memories will surface. For many of
us, our thoughts will gravitate primarily toward pretty darn good
memories, but for others, unpleasant memories may
predominate and become the basis for their stories.

Most of the stories by *TellTale Souls* that I have had the
privilege to read are delightful illuminations of small slices of
life. Some stories, however, either expose the dark side of the
soul or indicate a lack of connection to the soul-line in certain
folks who have caused the storyteller incredible grief and pain.
Thankfully, after completing their memoirs, the writers who told
heartwrenching stories inevitably came to places of better
understanding about the people who'd inflicted misery on them.
Rather than continue to lay blame on themselves for the bad
behavior others directed towards them, many thoughtful writers
came to the conclusion that the perpetrators had unbalanced
spirits, dispositions that were a reflection of their inner turmoil.
The storytellers learned not to "own" the problems.

Looking at both sides of the soul is worthwhile, since
lessons for living a life laced with wisdom teach us to distinguish
dark from light and how to deal with the ever present shades of
gray. Our memories create complex images that take some
sifting and sorting, but we will be glad we took the time and
energy to carefully examine them. There is redemptive power in

taking a second look at memories when we do so with open mindedness and the intention to discover the truth.

There will undoubtedly be lumps and bumps as we travel memory pathways. Suffice it to say that is the nature of memory. We will recall poignant memories that bring lumps to our throats and tears to our eyes. There will be bumps in the road, even roadblocks, due to the mysterious machinations of the mind when attempting to bring stored moments in time clearly to the forefront of our consciousness. We also block certain images because our scheming subconscious wants to keep us in the dark. Could we do without the lumps? Well, not really, they are inevitably part and parcel of the journey, so we will examine them and smooth them out as best we can through our powers of discovery. What's more, working through intricate obstructions provides insight that otherwise may have stayed hidden from view.

Perhaps even more than delighting in pleasurable memories, it is beneficial to write about the memories that make us uncomfortable. Through the act of writing, clarity and understanding come, and with clarity and understanding the stage is set for healing. Countless books and articles have been written on the subject of the healing aspects of writing. The cathartic effect of writing is well documented in literature, and I have quoted some of the positive firsthand experiences *TellTale Souls* have had with their lumps and bumps. Even in the best of relationships with our mothers, there are times we remember that are not so good. Tough times are valuable and worthy of exploration, because they have a way of continuing to impact us psychologically throughout our lives.

CATHARSIS

Catharsis is a psychological release brought about after bringing repressed, often intense, emotions and feelings to the surface in an effort to identify and come to grips with them through greater awareness and comprehension.

In your effort to deal with difficult experiences and go to places where you don't know everything, writing *Mother Memoir* is an invaluable process toward understand and healing the wounds of the past.

Working with pen in hand through dark memories with as much honesty as you can muster is one of the most cathartic exercises of which I am aware. A note of caution: Seek guidance from medical or spiritual professionals at any time you feel overwhelmed or just need to talk through experiences as they arise.

QUICKLY WRITE a list of five good memories and five unpleasant memories about a mother figure that come to you immediately— don't think too much about it. Then write a paragraph on each of them. Of the five good memories, note the predominate emotion you connect to it. Do the same with the five unpleasant memories, but now also note whether you believe exploring them fully could result in emotional release.

Whether your story is filled with light and happiness or misery and regret, there's no denying a significant relationship that holds power over you. Recognize, respect, honor that power. If you experienced a difficult relationship with your mother, you may hesitate writing a bio-vignette—balk at the very idea. This is a good time to appreciate the idea that what I mean by encouraging *TellTale Souls* to honor others through story, includes honoring the influence of relationship. Realize the lessons in the guidebook provide an opportunity to take a step back and look closely at your mother as an individual in the context of your relationship.

The *Mother Memoir* is a powerful vehicle to write through the known and the unknown. It's an avenue toward better understanding yourself and others, and it is an honoring by simply taking the time and energy to write about another individual who, for whatever reasons, has a hold on you through memory.

Writing a memoir is like making your way through a maze. You will go to places where you do not know everything; you are not sure if you should venture right or left or backtrack some, but then you realize this journey of mystery and suspense is exactly where you want to be. It is hard to back away from life's events and experiences to see them clearly because you have invested years of time and energy believing what you thought was so was so. The harder it is to let go of memories that you feel in your gut are misshapen, the better—I did not say easier—it is for your well-being to reassess them. The honest attempt to put your ego and emotions aside is the frame of mind essential to writing bio-vignettes that capture the character and spirit of your mother.

This is a reminder for all of you who write memoir or are beginning to write memoir. Question your assumptions rather than singing along with the same old tune that has been running in your head for years. To take this one step further, even after you have backed away to get a better view of the events or experiences you are writing about, the way in which you remember them will also differ greatly from the way someone else "clearly" remembers these same incidents. Listen to what others say, if it is important for you to do so, but hold fast to your questioning mindset. Their reflections could nudge additional memories out into your consciousness, but realize that what you see clearly is your truth. Rely on this without second guessing.

> **WRITE** two pages about an incident that you remember well, but you have heard a different take on that same incident from someone else who was there at the time it happened. Write from both perspectives to see if you can get down to the crux of the difference in opinions. Has this exercise changed your assumptions or perceptions?

TAKING YOURSELF BACK IN TIME

So let's get to work. Settle in, relax. You are about to embark on a stimulating journey where you will come up on ideas and happenings swiftly and unexpectedly. You will renew connections with old memories, strengthen links to memories lying dormant, and discover new meaning in memories you had previously not fully appreciated. If this is your first attempt at writing memoir or even if you have had plenty of practice, the activities and exercises we will cover together in the pages that follow will open the door to new and promising possibilities and perceptions. *TellTale Souls* tell me they've experienced flashes of sudden comprehension as they grasped the significance of memories in moments of truth when tapping memory using this method to write.

From the exercises you have completed thus far, you have toyed with many memories associated with your mother, grandmother, or another mother figure, so I imagine you know who will be at the center of your bio-vignette. If you are not sure, choose someone—you can always decide to write about a different person later on. This choice is not etched in stone. I am reminded, once again, of the student who was definitely not going to write about her mother—too painful—so she chose her grandmother to pay tribute to. Although, as soon as she finished the story about her grandmother, she immediately plunged into dealing with the painful issues surrounding her relationship with her mother; the very same mother she said she would not go near with pen and paper. Never say never.

You know whom, now what? Which memory best answers the seminal question: *If you could tell just one small story that would capture your mother's character and keep her spirit alive for generations to come, what would it be?* Don't worry, you are not alone if you haven't decided or even located the memory you want to use for your bio-vignette. This choice can be a tough one, perhaps the biggest decision some *TellTale Souls* come up against while on this journey. Almost everyone has a bit of anxiety over it—either they haven't found the absolutely *perfect* memory or they can't figure out which one of a multitude of memories to focus on. This can be one of the most difficult parts to get around, but only if you let it. Don't. Trust the process—go with the flow of your intuition—you really cannot go wrong.

Take a minute now to think about if there actually is such a thing as perfect. Certainly no one is perfect, not even—perhaps especially not—your mother, so take it easy on yourself. Inevitably, you will find satisfaction in the fact you've found the most fitting memory to use to tell the tale.

WRITE one page listing your mom's perfect, okay, best qualities and a sentence or two describing each of them. Decide as you write whether you find these qualities interesting enough to develop into a story. Now write one more page identifying and describing her worst qualities, and will they hold interest in story form. Imagine what would happen if you combined the best qualities with the worst to add tension to your telling tale.

You are possibly feeling a bit of tension right now in the form of pressure that you are exerting on yourself to get "it" right, even though I have suggested you relax into the process. Well, I see that as a good thing, since what you're feeling is not only understandable, it is fortunate. This type of tension will make you more alert to the signals you will receive while bringing memories into focus and attending to the details of writing well. I mention tension here, right before we go into a time of reflection followed, by a quick-write exercise, because I want you to be ready to act on any and all signals that present themselves, whether they make sense to you at the time or not, and so that from here forward you will look for details about your mother that will add tension to your story.

TENSION

Tension is felt as a mental, physical, or emotional strain, and it is not always a bad thing. On the contrary, tension and suspense go hand-in-hand with good writing. In fact, using tension is an excellent way to keep yourself astutely aware of the writing process, your story telling, and your readers reading.

To create tension, for example, let small gestures or contradictions of character convey a sense of contrast in your mother's personality. Choose dialogue that asks questions and begs an emotional response or leaves the reader in suspense for a time. Let tension float in your story for awhile before it is resolved, whether that amounts to only a couple of story lines, or it is reflected in gained wisdom revealed at the climax and/or conclusion of your bio-vignette.

INNERSEARCH

Innersearch begins as a conscious, truth seeking effort into the subconscious realm whereby discovery and appreciation of your mother's true character and spirit supports understanding of that most basic relationship. As a *TellTale Soul*, you will use this essential, enhanced memory technique to tune out the outside world and move inward in search of memories and their meaning.

Innersearch is not a time or place for intellectual thought. It is a state of being. It is a place to first simply allow an opening into the subconscious mind through a willful intent to disallow judgment and reasoning. *Innersearch* further develops as a process through which the feelings and emotions connected to people, places, and incidents can be purely taken in at a deep level. Any new awareness that occurs can then be contemplated and integrated into your consciousness.

Using *innersearch* as a prelude to a quick-write is rewarding. You'll soon see what I mean, as you follow along with the relaxing and energizing plan I have in store for you. Don't try to intellectualize or out-think it. Relax and bring along just enough tension to make the ride interesting and pleasurable. Plucking juicy memories comes naturally when you use *innersearch* to surf the realm of the unconscious mind. Now is the time to get focused and tune into your memories. You will need some uninterrupted time for this, so plan accordingly.

The following simple exercise will help you shift your focus from the day's events and that pesky conscious mind that tirelessly races hither an' yon. After doing this exercise for five to ten minutes (or for as long as you want—you be the judge), open your eyes slowly and list a few words describing the picture or images you have formed of your mother during this *innersearch* and how you feel or relate to the imagery.

- ➤ Make yourself comfortable—soundproof rooms aren't necessary!
- ➤ Keep writing tools within reach so you can take notes whenever the spirit strikes.
- ➤ Take a moment to *pause* and *reflect* on your objective.
- ➤ Consciously begin to exclude the outer world.
- ➤ Close your eyes slowly so that you are aware of the shades being drawn—your sight receding.
- ➤ Take a couple of slow, deep breaths and simply sink into your being . . .
- ➤ As you exhale, breathe out all mind chatter, allowing yourself to move from exterior surroundings.
- ➤ Each time you slowly inhale, breathe in her essence—draw her into the center of your being—begin to bring her image or something about her into your mind's eye—bring her being into the forefront of your mind.
- ➤ Just sit with the simple act of breathing—what a

marvel—breath *is* life . . .

> Don't force anything, stay in the moment.
> If the images you are evoking don't soon come in, go back to celebrating your breath, let it fill you up, take over—place any unwanted thoughts and images on your breath and exhale them away.
> Breathe slowly in, slowly out, moving further inside with each breath . . .
> Allow memories their space, welcome them.
> Let memories from your subconscious mind fill your consciousness.

This is a potent way to get in touch with your memories or seek answers to questions; it works every time, just as long as you don't get in your own way. Allow something special to happen in your relationship with your mother. And remember there is always tension in any relationship—make it work for you.

QUICK-WRITE: Don't stop to think, analyze, or judge, just write fast—what comes to mind the moment your eyes are open, which images took you by surprise or raised your temperature or your hackles? Pick up a pencil or tap the keyboard filling the page(s) with whatever materializes. It doesn't need to make sense. You will make sense of things further down the road.

> Write It   > Draw It

> Sing It   > Feel It

> Take specific note of how or what you are feeling.

The notes you make as your journey progresses are important. Save them. You may not use them right now, but you will revisit them as your story evolves and understand their significance later on. Memories have a way of connecting with other stored memories as well as with immediate thoughts and emotions. Think of them as the bread crumbs Hansel and Gretel scattered on their way to the gingerbread house—they will prove to be invaluable to you, too.

For some of you, a fountain of words might be flowing out after this first *innersearch*. One woman told me that during her *innersearch* a story began to come more quickly than she could write it down. To compound matters, she was hearing the story in German and translating it into English as she wrote— wouldn't we all like a "problem" such as that? She was not complaining; she felt very satisfied. If this happens to you, climb aboard and ride it to the end.

The quick-write is a good exercise to use often. You will begin to get more and more uninhibited the more you work with this writing tool. Also, take note of the value you find in this assignment. Our minds are amazing. The saying goes, "Use it or lose it." So to prevent losing your mind, use it—this time without direction! Let it run free and easy. The exercises and activities in this book are meant as tools for you to use as a guide. You may deem some of them more appropriate than others. I hope you will twist them, turn them, change them to your liking.

Continue to delve into the memories that come up for you during reflective times, day dreaming, or when they pop up out of the blue as you go about your day. It's your job to extract meaning from particularly revealing and intense moments. The next exercise, a couple pages forward, involves answering deep questions about the meaning behind memories. It's both interesting and informative, but you may want to skip it for now and come back to it after your story is near completion.

My sister Dana found it worked better for her to look for the meaning later. I asked her to explain: "My biggest difficulty was starting. A struggle went on between my heart and my mind. I was analyzing and intellectualizing memories rather than just going with them. There was one memory that crept into my mind over and over again that seemed insignificant—trivial really—until I let my heart take over. After spending time with that seemingly trivial memory, it became the theme for my memoir about Mother. Had it not been persistent, and had I not sensed its significance, I would have let that memory get away. It was through the journey of writing that understanding came."

Pot O'Gold

~Dana Johnson

I perched on the top of the red stone steps in front of our house, watching the final drops of rain dripping from the autumn leaves of the giant oak tree. My mother's beautiful alto voice rose and fell softly, filtering through the walls of the house. "You are my sunshine, my only sunshine. You make me happy when skies are gray…"

It was a lazy Sunday afternoon, and as she sang, the rays of the sun glazed the clouds, spreading shadow and light in patterns across the lawn. It was then that I knew for sure my mom was special. She believed in the pot o' gold at the end of the rainbow and in leprechauns and tooth fairies and Santa Claus, and now she had called out the sun.

The draw of the rainbow beckoned me. We had always gone together, as a family, to find the gold, but I was a big girl now and I felt sure I could find it on my own. After all, I could cross the street. I always looked both ways. So, I skipped happily along the sidewalk—never ever stepping on any cracks of course—humming my mother's tune. I knew the gold was there, where the colors touched the earth. I walked for what every young child believes to be a very, very long time. So long, that finally I saw the sun edge into the western sky, and the rainbow began to melt. I knew I had to go back. Once again, I had not reached it in time. But it was okay because, as my mother always said, there would be more to come. "Be patient, Dana."

I walked back to the house and climbed up to the porch listening for the sounds of Mother. Nothing. Tippy-toeing into the kitchen, I came across a note that read:

"Dear Dana,
We went to find the pot o' gold at the end of the rainbow.
Will be back soon.
Love, Mother"

I was crushed. She had taken my brother and sister and gone to the end of the rainbow—without me.

The rain still softly dripped from the oak leaves and the top step on the porch still held me as I sat alone, my head resting in my hands, waiting. The tires of our car crunched the gravel as my mother parked it at the side of the house. My brother and sister tumbled out, and my mother's soft blue eyes twinkled with glee as she scooped me into her arms and dropped three golden chocolate coins into my hand. My mother had really been there—right to the pot o' gold. I wasn't surprised, really. After all she knew where it was.

~~~

Encircled by the roses on the crematory grounds some forty years later, I reflect on my life's journey, still trying not to step on the cracks, away from but always back to the essence of my mother's gold. I turn slowly, with my sister and my husband in tow, raise my face to the sky, the sun, the oak trees, and catch her ashes in my hands, feel them settle on my body, trying to inhale all of her. She has made her final journey to the end of the rainbow without me. But it's okay. She taught me how to find it before she left.

Photo contributed by Dana: Waiting on the front porch, again.

Dana Johnson: "Writing my story didn't change my perceptions of Mother; I found it encapsulated her beauty."

To fully appreciate the impact images have on you and to begin your job of pulling meaning from remarkable memories and those you have not yet considered significant, ask yourself the following questions in conjunction with the quick-write exercise you completed a few minutes ago.

ANSWER by writing out your responses to each question briefly, but mindfully:

Why did a certain memory enter my mind?

Has this memory come to me in the past?

If so, why do I think I revisit it on occasion?

Have I communicated with this memory?

Do I invite an interchange or dialogue with this memory?

What is the reason certain memories make me joyful, make me sad?

Throughout our lives we stash away little secrets, sudden flashes of events, and certain things we intuit about people but have not consciously realized until we seek awareness, let go, and summon them. You may not know the meaning of vivid memories until you explore them through writing. It is through the process of writing that you will know and better understand the person you are writing about and yourself. Have you ever stopped to wonder who she really is? I can guarantee you will discover that you actually know more about her than you think you do, and what is more, further information will be revealed about her once you take yourself back in time and look ever so closely while asking yourself, "Who is Mom at her core, as an individual?"

Who is your mother? **WRITE** two pages about whom you think your mother is as an individual. Write one more page about whom you think she thinks she is. Do you see a contrast between the perspectives?

LOCATING AND ORIENTING

By now you have had ample opportunity to practice searching internally, so you have a good idea what works for you when you want to call forth the essence of your mother. Isn't it great to know this experience is available to you anytime you wish to retreat from the external world? And there is no end to the places you can visit next time you journey inward. There are hundreds of ways to locate significant memories. We'll start with a few. To make this adventure more interesting, take a thoughtful look at the places I have listed below, even, if at first glance, they don't resonate with you, they may be triggers...

> Where were you raised or where did you spend blocks of time?

City	Town	Suburb	Countryside
Desert	Woods	Mountains	The Outback
High Seas	Prairies	Ski Village	Military Base
Cabin	Near a Lake	By the Ocean	Tent

> What was present in your neighborhood?

Skyscrapers	Alleyways	Backyards
Friendly Neighbors	Distant Strangers	Pastures
Flowers Blooming	Birds Tweeting	Fish Jumping

Animals Roaming Freely or Leashed

Bicycles, Balls, & Bats—Welcome or not?

➢ Was your home a house, an apartment, or something altogether different?

Brick	*Clapboard*	*Stucco*
Mud Walled	*Animal Hide*	*Packed Snow or Ice*
Ranch Style	*Log Cabin*	*Highrise*
Tin	*Opulent*	*Meager*

Explore the interior of your childhood home or your current abode—note particular places or rooms that hold *emotion*.

> Place yourself firmly and reflectively in a room of your choice in your home by using the *innersearch* exercise you learned in the last section. Then **WRITE** one page filled with the emotional sensations that arise while linking them to the images and events from which they developed. Travel from room to room and repeat this process in each place your mind takes you.

Look at yourself at different ages or various stages in relationship to your mother—find significant *feelings*.

> Place yourself firmly and reflectively at the age of thirteen in the context of interaction between you and your mother by using the *innersearch* exercise you learned in the last section. Then **WRITE** one page filled with the feelings that arise, while linking them to the images and events from which they developed. Travel to other age related interactions between you and your

mother and repeat this process at each stage you visit.

➤ Which memories come to light when you think of your mom and—

Summers	*After School*	*Vacations*	*Television*
Movies	*Winter Evenings*	*Writing*	*School Days*
Illnesses	*Meal Time*	*Books*	*Working*
Love	*Serving Others*	*Dancing*	*Cooking*
Skiing	*Holiday Rituals*	*Gardening*	*Sleeping*
Exercising	*Social Media*	*Technology*	*Heartbreak*

Habits (endearing & obnoxious)

Leslie, one of the first *TellTale Souls*, wrote the following telling tale after exploring one busy room in her childhood home. This room was filled with poignant emotions which she found expressed volumes about her relationship with her mother. She achieved success in a mere 700 word bio-vignette.

La Toilette

~Leslie Sullivan

When I was a kid, the best part of the day was when mom and dad came home from work. They were happy to see us, and we were ecstatic to be with them. They were so big, larger than life, like two movie stars. I thought my mom was incredibly beautiful with her blond hair stacked in a beehive, high heels, and shiny painted fingernails. She smelled so good. It seemed like we eight children couldn't get enough of her. I believe that went for my dad as well. Mom was an only child, and she used to tell us she thought it was neat having so many people to love and to love her.

After dinner one night, I had finished my homework and went searching around the house for Mom. I wanted to know where she was at all times. When I came to the main bathroom, I noticed the door was slightly ajar and the bath water running.

"Mom are you in there?"

"Yeees."

"What are you doing?"

"I'm going to take a bath."

"Can I come in for awhile?"

Permission was granted. And so we entered into a tradition that continued for many years.

As a six-year-old, I was the perfect audience filled with awe and a million observations and questions. She filled the tub with bubbles and perfumed oils, and I sat and chatted with her as long as she would have me. It always seemed as if she were preparing herself for something beautiful. After she sank into the deep water, she explained that she put a washcloth across her chest to keep warm. I recall thinking she was hiding from my bulging eyes as I was struck by the sight of her womanly body. But I took her at her word about the washcloth, and I believed her promise that my body would one day be more like hers.

I questioned her about this cream and that sponge. I watched with intensity as she soaped her legs with the shaving brush and pulled the razor slowly across her white skin. What was that strange stone she used to scrub her feet? Why did she put that jelly-like mask on her face? Why did she use a stick on her toenails? My questions were never-ending. With infinite patience she explained to me that I would need to do these things as I grew up to feel better and to take care of my body. Sometimes I scooped up a handful of her bubbles and pretended to shave my legs. She told me how to avoid cuts by holding the razor just so. I wanted to do all the things she did, but she said children were so perfect that we didn't need beauty routines. I was determined to practice anyway. As I became more accustomed to the routine, I would run her bath and lay out all the toiletries, as though she were my queen. Often our time while she bathed was spent just talking about our days. It was a quiet time. A time I could just be with her while absorbing the secrets of womanhood.

As I grew older, the rituals of her bath had become less mysterious, but the bath was still a sanctuary where we could have much-needed private conversations. I grew aware of her need for privacy, so we all (for the idea caught on like wildfire with all of my sisters) popped in and out for short powwows, conflict resolution, or for help with our homework. But when Mom went back to school, we were invited to the tub again where we quizzed her for her exams. We took turns going through stacks and stacks of flash cards for her Spanish, biology, and literature courses.

Looking back I realize Mom was giving me and my sisters perhaps the only time she had to herself in the entire day. Today I don't think I ever take a bath without remembering my mom's bathing. And if I place a washcloth across my breast, I feel an overwhelming sense of comfort.

Photo contributed by Leslie: With Mom on the Merry-Go-Round

Leslie Sullivan: "I looked for the big experience with my mother to write about, but found bits of time was the vital element. Living in San Francisco for over 40 years, with most of my seven siblings, parents, and friends, I do my best to give valuable time to each of them often. It's the little connections that ultimately make the most difference."

Pre-teen Samantha's story brings up more memories of how precious are the simple times mothers and daughters spend together. This little *TellTale Soul* noticed that she had a good thing going. It's also one of those universal stories to which mothers the world over can connect.

Read Me

~Samantha Kirchhoff

The last thing my mom and I used to do before I went to sleep each night was our most special time together. But to get there we went through a few stages, while I was growing up. Long before I can even remember, and up until just awhile ago, my mom would cuddle in bed with me each night for about half an hour of reading. Then she'd silently wait until I was fast asleep so she could finally sneak out of my room, hoping I wouldn't wake up. I called this "read me to bed," which shortened over the years to just "read me." My dad took turns with Mommy "reading me," and my big brother and sister had some turns, too, but it was mostly Mommy.

"Read me to bed" changed as I changed. After I learned to read, my mom encouraged me to read out loud to her, so I'd get some practice with my reading skills. But when I was through with my story, I still needed to hear the sound of her voice reading to me. I liked the way her voice rose and fell as she made the stories more exciting, and I loved the funny or scary voices she'd use to make the characters sound real. I never seemed to outgrow my need for this, but "read me" eventually progressed to each of us reading our own books silently, side by side, in my bed. As I grew older, after the last of my reading for the night and a final hug and kiss, the second I turned over to go to sleep questions would start popping into my head or I'd think of other things that had happened during the day that I just had to tell her. She was still there, of course, reading to herself and waiting patiently to hear my

sleeping breath so she could sneak out. I just couldn't go to sleep until we'd talked about everything on my mind, so I'd open my eyes, and we'd talk for awhile. Usually finding something to giggle about. We never forgot to have fun.

By the time I was about ten, Mommy was getting pretty tired of "reading me to bed" because she'd get so warm and cozy and comfortable in my bed and then have to move to her own bed, after I'd fallen asleep. That's when a new ritual took shape that still exists today—with a twist.

This latest ritual is referred to as "tuck me in," and it has never included anyone else—only my mom could tuck me in. It was still our special time, and it didn't take nearly as long as "read me" did. It was, in some ways, a game—one that I usually won. Before I started getting ready for bed each night, I would say, "Mommy, don't forget you have to tuck me in."

Then she said, "You'd better hurry up. I'm almost ready for bed, and I'm not going to wait for you, I'm too tired."

That's when I turned into Speedy Gonzales and got ready as fast as I could (either that or I'd find a way to slow her down so she wouldn't be ready so soon). When we were both finally ready for bed, I called from my room, "Okay, Mommy, I'm ready, tuck me in."

Then she predictably replied, "You'd better be in bed and ready to turn off the light by the time I get in there." (Which meant that I needed to already have my alarm set, have my covers all perfect, and have my Carmex on).

She'd come in and sit down next to me on my bed for what I think she imagined would be about thirty seconds, but what turned out to be ten minutes—if I was lucky. I held onto her hand so that she couldn't get up easily and leave, and we hugged and kissed. With her smooth, white cotton nightgown, or delicate flannel pajamas, she was always so soft and cuddly, welcoming more hugs. And no matter how cold it was under my sheets when I got in, she brought warmth.

That's when, as usual, I remembered things I'd wanted to tell her or ask her advice about earlier, so I started talking up a storm. We laughed and talked for a while, and then she "remembered" that she was supposed to go to her own bed awhile ago, and she tried to get up and leave. But I almost always could get her to stay a little bit longer with the excuse that I had just remembered something else or that I just needed one more hug and kiss, including our special Eskimo or butterfly kisses. When I finally let her…she switched off my light, and I went to sleep happy with the thought that I knew she knew my tricks, but she puts up with them because she loves me and does her best to give me her time whenever she can.

Those extra ten minutes with my mom were the absolute best way to end each day. On rare occasions, when I didn't get ready quickly enough and she was exhausted or already in her own bed, I tippy-toed in to kiss her good night. But I didn't sleep as well if I had to crawl into bed without her "tucking me in."

I love you and I like you, too.

Photo contributed by Samantha: Reading to my best friend.

Samantha Kirchhoff: "I always liked listening to stories, especially from my Mom. But I also liked reading to my dog, Woody, when Mommy was busy."

The following are questions essential to the *Mother Memoir* process. We may have touched on some of them previously, but now that you have ventured a little further down your path to writing your bio-vignette, it is a good time to greet or revisit them.

Please, in each case below, CONSIDER FULLY and ANSWER THOUGHTFULLY IN WRITING. You be the judge of how much time and effort you are willing to give each question. They needn't be answered in any specific order:

1. Where and how do you find passion in your memories about your mother?
2. What thoughts, ideas, and actions link you inexorably to her?
3. What three words come to mind when you think of your mother?
4. What about her do you find most intriguing to include in your bio-vignette?
5. Which of her characteristics move you most?
6. When you look at a photograph, how do you imagine capturing the spirit and character of her being—finding those qualities not apparent in the photo?
7. Why do you want to honor or better understand your mother?

These questions can be weighty and complicated and deserve your full attention, so don't feel you need to answer them all in one sitting. You may change your mind several times while sorting out the answers anyway. Don't force this exercise; let things flow and be open to the unexpected. It is renewing and exhilarating to make new discoveries or validate what you already know but had not given much thought to lately or have taken for granted—oops!

Which thoughts have stayed uppermost in your mind or made the most impact on you during your work on the questions above? Open up a blank screen or turn to a blank page and decide to fill it free-style. Think of that clear space or page as a sponge that is waiting to soak up your thoughts and leave a trail behind marked by your words as they intersect with the page in a whole new way. You cannot force this one, either. Allow whatever comes in to be okay. Let spelling and the rules of grammar fly out the window and, if nonsense occurs, be at home with it, invite it in.

> **FREE-WRITE:** During this rousing 15 minute, non-stop exercise let words fall out of you that may or may not make sense to you while you are writing them. Point your mind in the direction of your mother and write down anything and everything that comes to mind.

After you have finished your free-write, put what you have written away for at least one day before you come back to it. It is through trying to make sense of obscurities at a later date that you will be able to more fully encompass the truth. Oftentimes it is just a word, an image, or a feeling that has come over you that is important for you to discuss—talk about it, share it, have some fun with it. The power of certain words is invigorating and, more than once, I have seen the idea for a story grow out of a single word.

After a time spent in reflection, a *TellTale Soul* jotted down one single word about her mother which seemed rather silly to her initially, although a plethora of emotions erupted within her. As she sat with the word "wash," she realized placing her mother in the center of her washday world was the one story she wanted to tell that would capture her mother's character and spirit as nothing else.

My Mother's Wash

~Colette Hosmer

My mom had the best wash in town—maybe in the entire state of North Dakota. In the 1940s and 50s, when every yard had a clothesline, the phrase "don't air your dirty laundry for everyone to see" was taken literally by many people, especially Mom.

Washday began at the crack of dawn each Monday morning when Mom rolled an ancient machine, saddled with two large metal tubs, from our unheated porch into the warm kitchen. The motor hummed as the rollers squeezed clothes from one tub to the other, and the windows soon frosted over as the kitchen steamed up. The odors of Hilex bleach, cooking, and wash water blended into one familiar and comforting smell.

I loved to shadow my mother on those days when my older sisters were at school and Dad was at the store. Mom and I shared secrets when we were alone together—like the unsung joy of headcheese sandwiches with mustard and liverwurst on buttered toast dunked into milky coffee.

Our clothesline stood outside the kitchen door. Four strong wires stretched between wooden posts that held a swing at one end and a Purple Martin birdhouse at the other.

Mother raised line-drying to an art form: Shirts, pants, and skirts were clothespinned at the seams, socks hung by the toe, and washcloths by two corners, never one. As it waved in the breeze, the completed masterwork of orderly colors and dazzling whites was a sight to behold. "Nothing smells better than line-dried clothes," Mom stated each washday. Never mind how her sun bleached whites caught the eye of each motorist and pedestrian who angled around our corner lot.

Mom dreaded the occasions when our neighbors' wash overflowed their clotheslines and they borrowed a line or two of ours. "Just look at that," she grimaced from behind our screen door, "hanging every which way, and those whites—gray as all getout." It wasn't unusual for those neighbors to leave their clothes on our line for an extra day or two, until a stiff wind had whipped the already unfortunate arrangement into a twisted, faded conglomerate.

Undaunted by winter and unwilling to give up the benefits of sun and fresh air, Mother draped her wet wash over the dowels of a wooden clothes rack and set it out on the steps, where it froze solid.

My sisters went to work at the store after school and on Saturdays, while I was left at home to practice the ironing ritual:

> *Lay out item to be ironed*
> *Sprinkle with water as you fold piece in on itself*
> *Roll up tightly*
> *Place snugly in plastic laundry bag*
> *Repeat*

After a couple of hours, the rolls were evenly damp and ready to iron. I watched and learned Mother's technique as she artfully worked the point of the iron around each button and into awkward corners without pressing in an extra wrinkle. As Mom talked, the changing position of the shirt on the ironing board and the momentary resting then springing to action of the iron seemed like one fluid movement. "I wouldn't be caught dead," she emphasized, "sending your father to work with his shirt collar crumpled and wrinkled, like some people's husbands." Not only were my father's shirts pressed to perfection, he made an even greater impression when he pulled out his pressed, whiter-than-white handkerchief to blow his nose.

But nothing lasts forever. Late one night Dad laid his poker winnings on Mom's pillow and, within days, a brand new Speed Queen washer and dryer gleamed from a corner of our kitchen. The big washtubs were moved to the yard where, on hot summer days, they served as kiddie pools and dog bathtubs.

A couple of summers ago, when my dryer broke down, I bought some wooden clothespins and strung a line across my small backyard. My dryer has long since been replaced, but the clothesline remains. I use it to hang out white cottons and sometimes sheets and pillowcases. Mother would be proud of my brilliant whites.

Photo contributed by Colette: Swinging on Mom's clothesline.

Colette Hosmer: "Writing this story was a joy, hard work but it gave me so much. I thought of a multitude of things about my mother, but her "wash" seemed more real than anything else."

If you are discussing your memories with family members who share similar memories, be careful. No two people see the same incident in the same way—so be true to the way *you* see each memory. Their memories are theirs, yours are yours; although, other people's memories of the same incident may add flavor to your bio-vignette, so keep an open mind.

SEEKING BURIED TREASURE

There are exciting places to go where memories linger longer. Some you'll find listed after the next story, others will flow out of your own imagination. The sheer joy of stumbling upon all but forgotten treasures in closets, cellars, and caverns stimulates our creative juices. And the poignancy found in listening to old records, tapes, and CDs or downloading music from by-gone eras, as well as reading letters yellowed by the years, moves us to reminisce and awakens the muse. The Greek goddess of memory dwells in the recesses of the mind. Our minds also work with photographs or snapshots by automatically applying a story to them so as to render them three dimensional, giving them life. They are a prime avenue to use when unearthing memories.

In your search for unforgettable memories, look on weather as your friend. Try walking outdoors immediately after a thunder and lightning storm, taking your writing gear to picnic by a waterfall, or listening to the action of the pounding surf to summon memories from the deep. The negative ions generated by Mother Nature charge the air you breathe and stimulate relaxation and memory, giving you an edge up with the *Mother Memoir* process. This isn't the time or place to go into the physics of it all, but I'll give you a story set in a cellar during a thunderstorm in West Texas, complete with a little ditty, strong emotion, and a dose of undying love.

Memories from Mama's Cellar

~Darla Curry

If you spent the night with Mama and the weather turned raw, you knew you would end up sleep-running to the storm cellar. Thunder triggered an adrenaline rush in Mama's brain. It thunders a lot in West Texas in the spring.

I always wondered whether genes or habitat caused Mama's naked fear of thunderstorms. Especially since her offspring, my Dad and his siblings, all had the same hankerin' for a hideaway when dark clouds gathered overhead. In any case, Mama and Papa farmed cotton, and since their daily bread depended on nature's goodwill, they possessed internal DNA pre-programmed to respect weather elements.

Mama, a seasoned sky scanner, needed no fandangled tornado warning system. The smell of damp dirt, a flash of lightning, and horizontal rain catapulted her into the ritual of collecting coats for everybody in the house and lighting the coal oil lamp. Then, the silent wait, until Mama sensed severe weather's deadly mood ready to strike. Next, the frantic dash, with biting rain and sometimes hail pelting us in the face.

Six feet below the surface, we huddled together listening to wailing wind and obscure objects peppering the tin-covered cellar door. Yet, thanks to Mama's tomfoolery, our foreboding quickly faded into enchantment.

A spark of lightning illuminated Mama's spirit. She ran on two Eveready batteries, mental acuity, and keen wit. Hitching these traits to a subterranean audience energized Mama to belt out nonsensical songs at a speedy clip:

Hay-rum-a-day-rum, a hey hi ho

Rumble-stick, a bumble-stick, a setback, a penny winkle

In came a nippy cat, Sing a song of kitty

Can't you ki-me-O!

Then she leaned forward, burst into laughter, and clasped her small hands together.

No one ever told Mama elderly folks have memory problems; one poem she had learned by heart, Tommy's Prayer, *about a little crippled cellar-dwelling boy, contained eighty-one lines.*

Papa, all of five feet, five inches tall, 140 pounds, dug this cozy cavern with a grubbing hoe and shovel and a dash of machismo. He had completed this majestic task at every house they had inhabited. It was mandatory to keep their marriage together.

Almost every farm house had a cellar, but none more utilized than Mama's. Mason jars, resting on crude, handmade shelves, showcased preserved vegetables of all kinds and colors, as well as scrumptious plums and peaches destined to star in Mama's rendition of Cobblers to Die For.

The calories Papa burned scooping out Mama's safe haven primarily gifted her tranquility; it soothed her nerves when suspicious clouds loomed overhead. Mama's tranquility was dislocated only once, as far as I know. I'm glad it wasn't a night when I slept over.

Mother Nature played a prank on Mama, caught her off guard, and blitzed the house with torrential rain and ferocious wind. No time for orderly preparation or lamp lighting.

Mama grabbed coats, Papa hurried to lace his shoes and snatch a wooden kitchen chair to take with him. They lunged into the black, drenched night, groping their way toward safety. Papa thought he had arrived first. Blinding rain distorted a form hovering over the cellar door that he believed to be the family dog blocking his entry. He gave the form a well-placed whack with the chair he held and yelled, "Git outta here!"

It turned out, the dog was Mama bending over to grasp the handle of the cellar door. Papa should've known he couldn't outrace Mama in a flight from foul atmospheric conditions.

The country phrase, mad as a wet hen, is far too mild to describe Mama's disposition as she extricated herself from the mud, unharmed except for her ego. Papa must have felt that the twister followed him right into the cellar. He never told what Mama said to him that night, but I doubt there was any singing or story-telling on the program. Mama may have assumed the role of the nippy cat that came in to teach Papa the meaning of a rumble-stick, a bumble-stick.

When I cast an anxious eye toward stormy skies, the melody to Hay-rum-a-da-rum echoes in my brain. I can still smell the kerosene lantern and see its flickering wick scatter the lamps shape across the musty, mud walls. I'd like to roll back time and spend one more night in the warmth and glow of that sunken refuge.

Yet, in truth, the cellar didn't render comfort—Mama's love and laughter did. Even sixty years later, when life yields thunderstorms, I feel her near my side.

Photo contributed by Darla: Grandmother Hatti "Mama" holding me.

Darla Curry: "I like to spot the blunders of ordinary life and weave them into humorous tales that offer the reader a chuckle and an uplift."

Anytime during your search, whether reading telling tales or working on your personal *innersearch*, when a memory stimulus hits a nerve write it down or draw a picture; you can come back to it later. If you don't write it down, it will be lost. Impressions are slippery little devils—you don't want to lose them. With pencil in hand, have an interesting time indulging in more ways to uncover the buried treasures of the mind:

> Pore over the family photo albums, looking for details and clues.
> Crawl into the attic to search among the forgotten treasures.
> Read old letters; don't forget to read between the lines.
> Listen to music that is in line with your ideas.
> Reminisce with your sister, brother, mother, cousin, or good friend.
> Touch objects that make you feel connected to the person you are writing about or hold special significance.

Material objects can be deceptive; they are often more than they appear to be on the surface. They can be storehouses bursting with the remnants of a lifetime of memories simply vibrating with feelings and emotions, waiting there to touch you as you reach out to them. Even though I took care of my mother for three years in my home before Alzheimer's disease took her completely away, many of her things were packed away. After Mom's death, my sister mailed a few mementos to me, among them was a deck of cards Mom had used for years to play Solitaire. I looked at them nestled in this box of trinkets, not paying them much heed. After all, Mom was not a card shark or anything of the sort; she would simply while away evenings playing Solitaire when her eyes were too weary to read. Soon, however, I picked them out of the box, drawn to them by the familiar waterfall on the front of each card, a bit blurred by an aging haze, but I was warmed by the thought that the water still continues to flow into a timeless ravine carved through the snow-draped, crowned-with-blue-sky Rocky Mountains. But the moment my fingers curved around those worn edges, soft with wear, I burst into tears. I was electrified by the stored energy emanating from them. Mom's energy through a deck of cards produced raw emotion in me that I would have never imagined could come from a deck of cards. From this trigger, I luxuriated in the pleasure of simple memories of Mom, mixed with sadness that she was gone, but satisfying nonetheless. Although, I would have loved to have had the opportunity to play a game of Double-Sol with her just once again.

A man told me there is no doubt in his mind that he feels to this day—a decade after his mother's passing—his mother's warmth and love radiating from a watercolor of lovely irises she'd painted for him decades ago. There is also something to be said about bringing someone to mind and just coexisting with her image without searching for specific memories, but rather waiting for them to come to you. I find this quote by author Stephen King to be true: "Memories are contrary things; if you quit chasing them and turn your back, they often return on their own." So be patient as you begin your excavation.

The stories by *TellTale Souls* are often based in simplicity, as you have observed by the tales you've read in this book. It's seldom the big events in life that take us to our knees, so don't try to search for what you might think of as an earth-shaking memory to write about. It is the elements of real life that carry the most weight. When you think about it, an impressive event like your mother winning the Nobel Prize would be something you would be very proud of to be sure, but what makes the most difference in a person's life turns out not to be those big events at all. Where her spirit shines most brilliantly and gives you glimpses of her core has more to do with day-to-day events.

It is her nurturing that you cherish and that strikes you as most valuable for a memoir: Her hand gently stroking your forehead when you were not feeling well; the tears she cried with you when you had a miscarriage; the bunny cake with licorice whiskers she baked for your fortieth—yes, 40th—birthday; the way she coached your baseball team; or how she taught you to be strong. On the other side of the coin, it may be her neglect of your basic need for love and attention, the anger she spewed out at you for dating someone she didn't approve of, or her laughter when you were humiliated by her behavior that warrants a telling tale.

While you're remembering interesting things about your mother, keep in mind that a memoir needs a theme or an event around which your short, true tale will be centered, unlike autobiography, which does not require this feature.

WRITE: Ask yourself what you want remembered about your mother. Draft a few paragraphs about one idea in particular or combine several memories together to get down how you see her character and spirit coming together in a bio-vignette.

So tell a true tale about her. It's real life that counts. It takes only one heartfelt memory of your mother to capture her character and spirit in a telling tale. Here are a few reminders to keep you on course:

- ➤ You want to crystallize moments in time.
- ➤ The stories *TellTale Souls* write seem to turn out stronger, have more verve and panache, when they are held to a relatively contained span of time.
- ➤ Tracing her history is not something you can accomplish in a short memoir, nor is that the focus of a bio-vignette.

You may well go on to write a book filled with her history, even the family history, after you have completed the short, true tale you have set out to write at the present time. You will need to have faith in yourself and trust yourself to do this work. We've spent time focusing on the message, next we will focus on you, the messenger.

TRUSTING THE MESSAGE AND THE MESSENGER

At this point, I trust you have found that special memory, the seed, from which your story will grow. Now we'll move into developing the *Mother Memoir*. The true belief in yourself that you can successfully write your telling tale, that you can make this memory come to life in full bloom in memoir, is enough to make it materialize on the written page. Of course, you must still provide the water and the vital nutrients, but I'll help you with that as we move along into Acts Three and Four. I hope, and again trust, your experience thus far flirting with memories, discovering who your mother is, and finding understanding for troubling memories, while sleuthing through hideouts along the way, has been a worthwhile endeavor—one that you will cherish for the insights you have received. If anything has got you stymied, you will grasp more about the art and craft of writing the *Mother Memoir* as you make your way along this journey.

We have now come to one of my favorite junctures. You probably feel your thoughts and ideas deserve to be listened to. Deserve respect. They do. But you may still be wondering if your story will measure up to your standards and be accepted for its truth and your honest rendition of how you want your mother's character and spirit remembered. You may wonder if you really got down to the core of whom she is and where you are able to reasonably capture her character and spirit in a genuine manner. I know this can be a frustrating time, but hang in there. You have come too far to let yourself and your mother down.

This section is all about trust and giving serious thought to you, the memory keeper and storyteller. Listen to the authentic little voice inside, the one no one else can hear, and place complete trust in yourself and your clear ability to author this piece of nonfiction. While it's true the leading actor in your bio-vignette is not you, without your singular memories of your mother the story could not come to life as it should. You are the

---

TRUST

TellTale Souls become trusted messengers of truth as they see it. They trust their memories to give them an accurate depiction of people and events, because they take care to look at their recollections from the vantage point of their mother's nature as well as their own.

Trust is a firm reliance on the integrity, ability, or character of a person. It is committing to the care or custody of another human being. Trust is bound together with confidence and belief.

Trust in your innate ability. Trust in this—if you can tell a friend a story, you can write a bio-vignette.

CAST OF CHARACTERS

Protagonist: This is your mother—the main character, around whom the central theme of your story revolves. Remember the protagonist could also be your grandmother or another woman who played a motherly role in your life. Think of "her" as the leading lady.

Narrator: This is you—the person telling the story. Through your writing you'll recount pertinent incidents and events, describe details that make the story come alive, and illuminate the character of your mother and a few other "extras" whom you may have chosen to add balance and punch to your story. Think of yourself as the script writer.

You have many shoes to fill in this piece of creative nonfiction, since you are also:

- Best supporting actor
- Director
- Producer
- Scene manager
- Choreographer

You get the picture. At times you will take your cues from your mother's actions, other times she'll take her cues from you, but ultimately you get the final say—they are your memories and it is your story after all is said and done.

best supporting actor—they also win Academy Awards. With the idea in mind that each character in the *Mother Memoir* is playing herself, not acting, what could be easier? And, don't forget the fact you are also the writer, the director, and the narrator; there will be no story without you. Some say metaphorically, "Shoot the messenger," because the message was not what they wanted to hear. However, Pollack didn't back down as he exposed the truth when he directed the 1960s film, "They Shoot Horses, Don't They?" You're not going to shoot anything here, not even your foot, but you are going to aim your trusty writing stick at the bull's-eye and produce a telling tale.

TellTale Soul Marie, the messenger of the story below, tells us about growing up with an untrustworthy, self-centered, and jealous mother who did not have her daughter's best interests at heart. Although Marie found she could not trust her mother, she learned to trust herself. Through writing her bio-vignette, Marie came to realize she had never truly owned or given adult perspective to her emotional responses regarding her mother's actions toward her. Marie chose not to add a photo.

The Red Ledger

~Marie Wells

*H*ers *was a jaunty step like spring was perpetually in the air, as she stepped from the streetcar in San Francisco, seemed like there was always someone nearby to tell her how she brightened their day. My mother, the woman with the hourglass figure, raven hair, and smiling eyes of azure blue. The belle of the ball with personality plus, you can bet her dance card was full to overflowing.*

This is an apt description of my mother, but this was not the vision I have of her—this is not the mother I knew. No, the very word, mother, makes me shrink. Surely doesn't conjure up images of flowers and sunshine, home cooked meals, a smile just for me—her mirror image. My mother out in the world exuded a kind of magnetism, drew people in toward her charms, but turned it off, this magic, the moment she was alone with her family.

Perhaps the fact that I looked just like her accounted for her ill-treatment of me, her emotional neglect and outright contempt. Or maybe it was because she couldn't forgive me for not being a boy. She'd lost her first child, a darling baby boy, ten months before I was born. A daughter born to take the place of the son she'd lost didn't do the trick. Things may have been okay between us when I was a baby and a very young child, but they were not good for me during the Depression years. Now that I look back, things may have been not so good for my mother, either.

My father managed a stocks and bonds house in downtown San Francisco. My parents had purchased their first home and outfitted it smartly with overstuffed sofas (I can't believe this kind of furniture is back in vogue) and hardwood occasional tables with satin finishes. Our little stucco house with arched doorways and a curved stairway out front was one of the earliest homes built in the tract just up the hill off Ocean Avenue. My mother thought it was grand.

Then the stock market crashed in '29 and, with it, my father's job and spirit. He simply collapsed into the whole thing. My mother didn't think things were so grand then (who would?), as she packed us up, and we started to move from one flat to another over the next eight years. As the Depression years dragged on and on, we moved more and more often, down and down, until finally we were over in the Haight-Ashbury district. That was the low point. The year I was in the eighth grade we were in a building of three flats on the corner of Masonic and Haight streets, where the streetcars turn. The building is there today; I'm glad I'm not.

My mother became a raging bull. She alone would save the family. Monetarily speaking, she did. My mother, having only an eighth-grade education, went to night school to learn stenographic skills, so she would be employable. I chalk it up to her rebellious energy that she got work. It was the Depression, after all; times were tough. Throughout my teenage years, she had many jobs, from the switchboard at a local radio station to secretary for Sigmond Stern (a grove is now named after Mr. Stern in Golden Gate Park) and seemed pleased with herself. She had a flair for style and managed to look picture perfect for work. To this day, I don't know how she did it on her meager income.

She was resourceful; I'll give her that. Along the way when we were having all these problems—Depression troubles, that is—Mother began to write poems, jaunty little rhymes. She'd write catchy verses about the virtues of various products like jams or jellies or canned vegetables, send the jingles to those companies, and, like as not, in a couple of weeks a case of green beans, peach preserves, or bathroom tissue would arrive at our door.

She treated boxes of hand-me-down clothing as though a fairy godmother had spun them up especially for me. She dealt with all things like that as wonderful. It was wonderful to have the Masons bring us a turkey for Thanksgiving. It was wonderful to have the UCSF dental students fill my teeth and to go to the free clinic when I had an earache.

My mother knew how to work the angles. She was the buffer between me and the reality of how poor we were. That is something. But it was anything but wonderful when, for my birthday or Christmas, she would buy me several darling skirts with sweaters to match or a couple of stylish dresses only to take them all back the next day, saying she had decided that I didn't really need them or that I "looked terrible" in them. She did weird things like that, things that crushed me. Her ways and her words kept me always off kilter. I'd be dressed for school or to go out with friends, and she would just look me up and down and say something like, "Where's your girdle?" or "Is that the way you're wearing your hair?" I asked her once, after it dawned on me that only I was outfitted in drab and dark clothing, why was it that she got to wear such pretty, bright colors. "Who wants to look dull all the time?" she smirked. Looking back, I can only suspect she wanted to keep the younger, "spitting image" of herself in the background.

But more than anything else, I'll never understand her red ledger book. What sort of mother would keep a detailed record, complete with dates and dollars, of all the purchases she'd made for her child? On my wedding day, my mother presented me with the ledger, all totaled, and said, "I have spent this amount of money on you. What are you going to do about it?"

My hair has some white in it now, and the blue has faded a little from my eyes over seventy-some odd years. I'm told I still have smiling eyes. I know I still have emotional scars. I stole my mother's red ledger from her bureau drawer and destroyed it forty years ago. That helped some. Studied and was degreed in psychology; not sure if that helped or not. My mother died at the age of ninety-three, oblivious to the people and things around her. I hadn't seen her or talked to her for about fifteen years. But it was a shock, nevertheless, when I was notified that she was gone. Gone. What is gone? Something I never had is gone; so what is there to miss? When I closed that door back in 1971, I didn't turn back, but I suspect I hoped she might have called my name.

Marie Wells: "Telling this story was a good experience for me, and I've since done much soul searching and writing, exploring the negative experiences in the relationship between my mother and myself. I now realize that the pain around my relationship with her is gone. What I'm left with today is called health!"

Once you have the bones of your own story down, you will have an interesting time in the next two acts adding depth, design, and color, as well as finding ways to add the finishing touches to your memoir.

Consciously consider that only you, and you alone:

- ➢ have the capacity to write this important story.
- ➢ can add a certain color to your family tree by writing your specific story.
- ➢ have this unique experience of your mother.
- ➢ can see her from her vantage point, as well as your own.
- ➢ can hear a certain quality of her voice.
- ➢ feel her touch in just the way you do.

> **DESCRIBE**, by writing one paragraph on each of the points above, *how* you believe each one to be true and *how* you trust in your ability to write from your heart.

WRITE one full page on *why* you will write a story about your mother.

Because you have moved the *hows* and *whys* into reality, you know your voice is utterly unique and your story is invaluable. Now, we'll take a closer look at voice and where to find that powerful means of expression through which to channel your innermost thoughts and feelings about your mother into a true and telling tale.

DISCOVERING YOUR VOICE

It's there. Your voice. It is right there bubbling up inside you—you already knew that, didn't you? But do you believe it? Maybe you are thinking, "I just babble." Well, I think I babble on and on too, sometimes, but then I snap out of it and become coherent. You will find that very voice that knows what to say and how to say it so that the character and spirit of your mother will be revealed in your story. It is simply a matter of hearing the voice inside yourself and using it to guide your writing style. Speak from your heart directly onto the written page. No one but you can discover your voice. It is entirely up to you to find what's waiting there inside—awaiting your confidence and trust.

Simply put, voice informs memoir. It's the instrument you will use to tell your story. You are the narrator, the storyteller, and it's through your voice alone the story is told and controlled. The person who you are at this moment in time defines and creates the story, so your personal biases have a way of showing up. A word of caution: pay attention to personal biases sneaking into your story—they can get in the way of seeking the truth; we will go there in Act Three.

Using your distinctive voice, you will put together a short, true tale about things recalled as only you can tell it. How to recognize your voice and believe in the value of its inflections, undertones, and energy is pretty straight forward, but you also must have faith. Think of it this way, when you speak with friends on the telephone, it takes a word, a couple at most, for them to know it's you on the other end of the line—without looking at caller ID. You can achieve a similar tone on paper if your writing is authentically yours. Today when reading emails and text messages, it's interesting to note that people have unique mannerism and patterns in the way in which they get their messages across, allowing you to identify the person who sent the message even if the "from" area is blank. So, we have voice recognition and text recognition that don't require software or hardware programs, only our connectivity to each other—what a concept—human beings recognizing each other in spite of the technology.

Don't worry about whether there is a right way or a wrong way to use your voice to write your story. There is no such thing as the wrong way. How you choose to put into words your rendition of whom she is, at her core, is exactly as it should be conveyed. Remember this is an undeniably precious gift from you. It is a gift you are arranging to meet your needs, and you know it will be written in just the right way. So have faith and confidence in how your story will sound in your voice. Think of it as your golden opportunity to pay tribute to or to better understand your mother in a way that is intrinsically yours.

FREE-WRITE: Begin with a blank page to write in free-style as though you were telling this story about your mother aloud, without thinking about story structure. Talk to that page. It will listen. And it won't care whether or not your spelling and grammar are correct. It will readily absorb anything you've got to tell it. Write until you have exhausted the thoughts you have in mind up to this point, random as they still may be.

This exercise gave you the chance to be you. Being true to your real self provides vital authenticity and will give your bio-vignette its greatest appeal. Just think, no one else on earth has this special story to tell. I have heard it said, "Don't wait 'til the eulogy." Take this as sage advice—reflect on her character and spirit and write about her while she is still here, so she can enjoy the most valuable gift a mother can receive. And if she is gone, I believe she will still receive this message through you.

The following quotes are a few thoughts from *TellTale Souls* as they went through the process of discovery and writing their bio-vignettes:

➤ "By just starting the writing process and letting things flow, I can now find her without trying."

➤ "Not only did my grandmother's spirit come to life within me, while on this journey, but to viscerally experience my grandmother as if I *were* her was a profound experience for me."

➤ "It made me appreciate my mother as a person, not just how great a mom she was to me."

➤ "I was ashamed of myself for having thought I had nothing to say. And then I found out I had so much I needed to say to her, to thank her and honor her for who she is."

➤ "My relationship with my mother was difficult. What I'm left with today, after doing my story, is called health!"

➤ "I thought before writing the story that it wouldn't be interesting because nothing monumental stood out to tell about her, but I know now that it was the little things she did that were priceless."

➤ "Writing my story didn't change my perceptions of Mother; I found it encapsulated her beauty."

➤ "My mom is the greatest, now everybody will know it." (Delight in mom from an eight-year-old girl.)

➤ "I found out that she was really there for me even though I used to have it in my head that because she worked, she wasn't there. Now I don't feel guilty any longer that I, too, work and my children go to day care—they will get great things from me. That was a powerful lesson."

➢ "Writing this story gave a ghost some substance, and I discovered that my strength came from my mother."

Have you been writing, writing, and writing some more? You must—your story will not write itself. Steal away some time right now, put everything aside, including this guidebook, and get that story drafted. Let this be your time to let your voice be heard on the written page. Make this a time where you will drop self-criticism and doubt and immerse yourself in the story you are telling. Believe in the power of your distinct voice to convey this short, memorable tale. Someone now and in the future will appreciate your voice and be very glad you wrote this story.

WRITE: Complete your first draft of that *one* story you want to tell that would capture your mother's character and spirit as you see it. In this draft, include the basic elements of your tale in a form that has substance and flow.

You will learn to get craftier with your writing and continue to expand and mold your story in the acts that follow. Appreciate the fact that this is your first draft, and don't expect it to be all that you envision it to be just yet.

So as not to confuse the personality—tone, style, and tempo—of your subjective narrative voice, which is the primary purpose and center of attention in this section, we will take a quick look at other aspects of narrative voice. I am including this because many people think when I refer to voice my aim is to define what we learned in school regarding first, second, and third person, but that is not our concern here. You may have noticed, I shy away from laying down tedious rules—it's a lot more fun to write like we talk rather than worry about which "person" we are using to write heartfelt stories. That being said, most memoir is written in first person, unless you are writing your story in the form of a letter to your mother, be that prose or poetry.

Act Three

*O*ften times the end of the third act of a play signals the final curtain. Not so with us—Act Three is a time for actively engaging your energy in the realm of bringing your story to life. Your bio-vignette will mature as you focus on bringing in artful elements of design and creativity, engage your intuition, and flavor your story with imaginative elements that do not hamper truth.

I liken Act Three to the time in life when you have prepared your ground and settled into a productive plan and direction for the future. Even so, you may now find yourself questioning perplexing aspects of relationships and looking for the key to unlocking the mysteries inherent in memory. "Alice's Adventures in Wonderland" began with Alice falling down a rabbit hole and finding a key that opened the door to sorting out nonsense from reality. Her creative visions, although fantastical, added layers and depth to the tale and empowered her search for truth—Alice grew wiser.

ADDING DEPTH, DESIGN, AND COLOR

Now that you have mindfully given special memories the attention they deserve, found the raw material for your bio-vignette, and completed the first draft, it's time to lift the curtain on Act Three. In this section, your creative objective is to dig a little deeper and add some buzz to the details to enliven the *stuff* of life on a couple of levels: You want to find even more personal insight into this woman you call mother, and you want anyone reading your telling tale to appreciate the impact of her being.

Imagine yourself in the shoes of Lewis Carroll's Alice when looking for alternative realities for the thoughts you cling to surrounding mom and past events. Invite mom to join you for tea with the Mad Hatter to see if time is eternally standing still in the memories you keep—have you stayed stuck on ideas not rooted in reality—or will you move toward deeper awareness in the here and now? Putting fantasy faces on people and juxtaposing whimsical alternatives for the places surrounding actual events, as in Alice's journey, is an imaginative way to view things and will give you interesting ideas to toy with. You are writing a true story, so you won't incorporate fantasy characters, unless they are actually a part of how things actually were, but you can have some fun thinking along these lines, and you will gain insight along the way, as did Alice.

Simply looking at things in a different way allows creative energy to emerge. Adding depth to your story by design will also go a long way to arouse the interest of people reading your story. By incorporating even a smattering of words and adding imaginative elements, you will incite enthusiasm and bring vigor into your bio-vignette. As your emotions are stirred and you do your best to get your feelings across on paper, the result moves other people to feel the pull of empathy, regret, joy, sadness, love, anger, the entire range of emotions. If you are writing this story for future generations to get a glimpse of your mother's character and spirit or to relate to readers in general, remember you have to give them what they need—connection. They must feel a link or a tie between themselves and the characters when they read your story or they will simply stop reading your true tale—the one that means so very much to you. So decide what you want your readers to feel *before* you continue to write. What do you feel? Transfer those feelings as you write.

Take out the draft of your story, read through it quickly and ask yourself what you felt. **WRITE** two paragraphs describing these feelings in detail. Now pick your story apart a bit and highlight areas where you believe you could creatively design it to add depth and color.

I know from my experience working with people, as they begin writing, many of them have no idea what they want others to feel, let alone how they truly feel deep down inside, because their preconceived mind-sets get in the way until they take the time to delve deeply into complex feelings and let words flow from an inner source. Moreover, the idea about "how to touch others" did not occur to them prior to starting the writing process. So, from here forward, I am asking you to put the horse before the cart and spend time on what you want your readers to feel, as well as how you will bring about this transfer of emotion. Throughout this guide we will look at various devices useful in bringing about this desired effect.

Lynn Cook Henriksen

When you snap a picture with a camera, you might believe the details of appearance and elements of emotion on the faces and the body language of the people in the photo would be an accurate depiction—perhaps an easier way to portray their essence than in writing. But is this true? It has been said that photographs are an historical representation that is trustworthy. But can we trust this image? A woman told me she remembered taking a photograph of family members where the shot captured cheeks pressed to cheeks bulging with cheer and big smiles, but after the shutter was clicked, they backed off and resumed their bitter bickering. So much for that trusty photographic representation. Which do you think would be a more accurate interpretation of the group above, a story written by the woman who noticed the disparity between the pose and the reality of the situation or the photograph she snapped?

Photographs can be wonderful illustrations of physical reality, and I've asked you to go through family albums and use photos as tools to assist you in tapping into memories. You can go infinitely further than the camera goes with its one-dimensional reproduction because you can recreate with words the emotions and feelings radiating from the image you hold in your mind, heart, and soul. This is the time to fully recognize the value in capturing the character of individuals in a story as no photograph could ever do.

Describing details with words might not seem so challenging if you could point the viewfinder in the right direction and snap an honest moment in time. Well, this is exactly what you will do in your mind's eye, and the result will be your mental or psychological reality complete with your thoughts and feelings as a more dependable frame of reference from which to write. Point your energy and focus on each mental picture you want to bring to life and tell the page in front of you how these details look and feel, how they taste, smell, and sound.

In the first stages of writing as a *Telltale Soul*, Robin began to hear bits of melody and some of the words from childhood lullabies sung to her by her grandmother. Astonishingly, the songs floated into consciousness on the very voice of her grandmother.

Lullabies

~Robin Monigold

Dressed up in a gown that trails on the floor
In a picture hat your mommy wore
Living in a world that you never knew
My little lady, make-believe.

What a pair of shoes for two tiny feet
What a pair of gloves, the fingers don't meet
Posing in the glass, your joy is complete
My little lady, make-believe.

In your little arms a doll you enfold
Means the world and all to you
But you could never love the doll you hold
Half as much as I love you.

Dream your little dreams, may they all come true
May the coming years bring happiness too
All my future dreams are wrapped up in you
My little lady make-believe.

I need them—the lovely lullabies that were passed down from my great grandmother. Just a couple weeks ago, I asked my grandma to write them down for me. When I was a little girl, I spent a lot of time with my grandparents. I wasn't aware of it then, but now I see how very lucky we kids were that Grandma Edie and Grandpa Wayne lived only five miles from us in a suburb just outside of Dallas.

95

We spent so many memorable weekends with them, and sometimes in the summers we'd stay with them for weeks at a time. I loved most every minute of it, but my fondest memories revolve about our bedtime ritual with Grandma Edie.

Each night when it was time for bed, my grandmother would put my sister, Jamie, and me in the front bedroom, where we shared a bed. A twin bed. Jamie and I would crawl into our cozy little bed between the softest sea-green sheets that matched the sea-green carpet and the sea-green walls. We took turns as to who had to be squished against the wall and who was to be on the outside, nearest Grandma. We always took turns with everything at Grandma's house; I figure that's how she kept the peace.

Just as soon as we were snuggled in, Grandma clicked out the lamp adorned with a sea-green shade and got into that twin bed with us. We'd all three be in flannel pajamas in the winter and cotton nighties in the summer. She'd pull Great Aunt Bonnie's handmade calico quilt in around our shoulders, slide one arm under our necks, the other over the top, making sure to encircle us both in her arms. Then, in a whisper-soft soprano, she would sing the same lullabies to us that her mother had sung to her. But first, she never failed to promise, "I will sing to you until you fall asleep."

They were wonderful songs. We enjoyed them immensely. And with equal enjoyment, we anticipated what was to come, as Jamie and I always knew what was going to happen within the next ten minutes. Grandma would sing and sing in her soothing voice. But, after four or five of the lullabies, instead of singing us to sleep, she would have sung herself to sleep. This happened every single time. My sister and I would get so tickled seeing Grandmother fast asleep from her own lullabies that we would giggle ourselves to sleep.

When we woke up the next morning, she would be gone from our bed, having crept quietly in the middle of the night down the hall to the bed she shared with Grandpa. But how she left our bed at night did not happen in the same way each time. On occasion, I would be awakened by a very loud snore. Yes, Grandmother's snore. It was hard to believe this woman who had perhaps only an hour earlier sung to us in such a soft, melodious voice could be sawing logs with the best of them. Although she was asleep, I would shake her shoulder and tell her to get up and go to her own bed.

She wasn't hard to awaken, and Jamie slept through the snoring, but I was wide-awake. So I would lie there for the next little while, watching the lights from passing cars filter through the white sheers covering the window, rounding and retreating, rounding and retreating, and hum myself back to sleep with my favorite of Grandma's lullabies:

Robin is going to bye-lo-land

Going to see the sights so grand

Bye-lo, bye-lo, bye-lo-land

Robin is going to bye-lo-land...

I guess it's pretty simple, but I loved it.

My grandmother continued "singing us to sleep" until we were well into our teens. Even though, by that time, we had experienced the delightfulness hundreds of times, each time was as comical as the first. My sister and I invariably fell asleep with smiles on our faces.

Photo contributed by Robin: Grandmother's eyes saw the best in me.

Robin Monigold: "I'm now in my 40s and have recently graduated from nursing school. My grandmother was my mentor in living life. Specifically, she was the driving force to fulfill my dream to become a nurse. I wish she could have lived to see my dream become a reality. I now realize that if I hadn't written my story and asked my grandmother to write down the lullabies she sang to me as a child, those lovely lullabies would be forever lost. That would have been tragic."

How poignantly sweet are the echoes that start when memory

plays an old tune on the heart.

~ Eliza Cook

USING DESCRIPTIVE IMAGERY

Creatively describing images of characters and events in a story is how writers put into words the unique and lasting impressions that readers will connect with. You'll do this to add powerful appeal to your true story. As you saw in Act Two, the images I am referring to are the mental pictures you have stored away in your memory banks of a person, place, or thing, whether they are remembered vividly or remain in shadowy vision. Clear memories are, of course, more easily described if you get creative with your visions, whereas images in shadow are elusive. To run after a shadow and learn to describe it is exceptionally rewarding because you have brought a dim memory into the light and have become wiser for the effort. Using senses other than sight to describe a hazy image or using your imagination, coupled with what you do know, are good writing strategies. *TellTale Soul* Lynn Scott uses this approach as she weaves together her *Mother Memoir*.

I'm Imagining My Mother

~Lynn Scott

I am imagining my mother at three…a softly rounded little girl with huge blue eyes, set deep under lids like her papa's. Her hair a thatch of white-blond, wispy-straight hair kept tightly pulled back in bows or braids by fastidious Mama or fiercely serious Bestemor, her Norwegian grandmother who speaks no English.

99

Mabel is a bit pigeon-toed, and, consequently, knock-kneed. This causes her some awkwardness over rough ground; perhaps why, on this sunny day in New Jersey, she falls into the pit her father is digging. He has a deep voice and huge hands. One booms in a thick Nordic accent, "Didn't I tell you not to come near?" while the others plunk her miserable little muddy body back onto high ground where, with "achs" and "tish-tishes," Bestemor leads her to the bath.

I am imagining my mother at ten…still soft, but getting very tall with big-boned hands and feet. She and her family live in a house supplied by the Fort Lee Orphan Home Society. It is some miles away from the building bought "for the betterment of homeless children." Mabel and her sisters, Gertrude and Helen, have few things of luxury. So my mother's pleasure at receiving a surprise gift, a silver chain bracelet from their sea captain uncle— well—it is not just pleasure, it is giggles and blushing and thank yous over and over again. Her first piece of jewelry—she loves it!

But now it is evening, after supper and prayers. Her mother says, "Mabel, it makes you feel good to receive that nice bracelet, ya?"

"Oh yes," she rhapsodizes.

"So you know it is better to give than to receive, ya?"

"Yesss."…Now her joy steps back as she feels what is coming.

"Well, my dear, you know that Johnny in the orphan home has arrived without a good pair of shoes. He could have those shoes for the money your chain would bring. If we sell it, he will have shoes. Wouldn't God want that?"

She struggles painfully while her sisters watch wide-eyed. She knows she has lost. Who can win against God?

The three girls, perhaps 16, 14, and 12, sit around a tea table. The eldest sister Gertrude has her back to the camera; long cascades of slightly curled hair fall to her waist. She wears a casual skirt and a white blouse. Unlike the other two whose hair is still pulled severely into short and manageable styles, she seems to be on her way into that world outside. She holds up her cup. Helen, the youngest, head tilted like the teapot, is very focused on getting the tea into Gertrude's cup. Mabel, facing out from the curtained window wall behind her, holds her cup near her lips and is looking down into it. Bestemor must be dead. Her superstitious religion couldn't allow a soul to be snatched by the camera's image, could it?

I am imagining my mother at sixteen...Mebs (no longer Mabel), Mickey (no longer Gertrude), and Helen, the beautiful Boswick sisters, growing into the Flapper Age with all the attributes one needs—warm blue-eyed beauties. They are both eager and terrified to enter the world of dating. They have been taught that their bodies belong to God. They'd muddled into menstruation—a word they don't know. It is God's curse for Eve's sin of carnal knowledge. But there are opposing forces—their own ripe bodies, the sensuality of the 'twenties, and their mother's mixed message to wear lipstick, dress like other American girls, and be good girls.

I am imagining my mother at nineteen, flush with pride each time she looks at her likeness on the cover of Cosmopolitan, chosen by the illustrator from among many other girls. She keeps the magazine out of sight, not wanting a lecture about vanity, but the joy lasts among her sisters and friends. She is working now as bookkeeper in a Manhattan boutique and teaching Sunday school as a substitute for the church service that no longer holds her. She wears her abundant hair, slightly marcelled, looser now.

I am seeing you more clearly, my mother, twenty-three, standing in front of the big old Saddle River farmhouse where you brought me just after my birth. You are posing with friends stylishly dressed in the '20s short skirts, tight flat-chested bodices, legs turned ever so seductively, looking free from the old-time religion and all its limitations. I know now of the hole in your heart; the missing of the love of your life that your mother refused to allow because his father ran an Irish bar. I imagine it growing bigger by my father's quite public lusts after the endless stream of women drawn to this Eden where the bathtub gin flows freely in the barn.

Here you are at not quite 70, lying in a nursing home bed. "Oh Lynnie, you'll never guess what happened to me last night!" Your eyes are wide and your voice carries hair-prickling fear with a sly touch of fascination—a familiar prelude to sexual horror stories you fed me in my teens.

"I was lying here listening to that woman snore. Suddenly a priest came into the room and swooped me up from my bed and began walking out of the

room with me. But I told him we have a car in Ridgewood, and we know the Monsignor, and we will tell him. So he put me back in my bed and sneaked out." Ah, did you imagine it was your lost lover who, a lifetime later, returned for you too late?

I am reclaiming you, my mother, every facet of you. The chubby curious three-year old, the ten-year old with a healthy love of jewelry, the serious young Christian who early on found her shadow, the illustrator lifting you to the grand piano and toasting his favorite cover girl, the small town girl beloved (but not enough) by the dark and handsome father of mine; and yes, my mother, even the old woman whose disappointments splattered around me like sudden oil strikes, who, even at the end, questioned our rightness together. Forgive me please for loving you so late.

Photograph contributed by Lynn: Mother seeing me.

Lynn Scott: "I began writing seriously in 1988 at age 57. It began as an attempt to understand my place in my family of origin (very successfully) and culminated in three books and the crafting of pieces that have won prizes and appearances in several anthologies."

When you're describing images, say in a story about your grandmother, stop and really think about how you are communicating your reflections of her at a certain time, in particular places, and during specific events. Moreover, when you take the time to go through an exercise in descriptive imagery, you are allowing yourself to revel in depth about savored incidents.

When you're writing a memoir about your grandmother, for instance, ask yourself if you have made her, as well as your time with her, come alive through your depiction of the images you have perhaps carried with you since childhood. Have you conveyed to readers, through even a few words or a phrase, the emotional hold a certain memory of her had on you? Or is she coming across flat as a photograph, in a way that doesn't give her likeness or unforgettable moments the energy they deserve?

Descriptive, creative imagery will literally pull your story into a deeper dimension by showing, rather than telling, what you mean through words; words evoking mental images that allow people to connect with your characters on that emotional plane we have been talking about. For example, you could say, "I liked to go fishing with grandma early in the morning." Or you could say, "I had been shivering on the back porch for what seemed like forever, when suddenly my heart skipped a beat when I heard grandma open the creaky wooden door at the crack of dawn, two fishing poles geared up in one weathered, but not frail, hand." Both of these sentences have the same meaning, but the second one pulls readers into a visual of you and your grandmother at that precise moment you want remembered.

Action is created by your choice of words. You may want to play around with different ways to portray specific images, feel the emotional responses your descriptive images can evoke, and then decide what you will say to achieve the results you're looking for.

There is a side to adding imagery to be wary of, however. You don't want to overdo it by overwhelming readers with descriptions that take away from your story line. Take this cliché to heart, "Can't see the forest for the trees." Your memoir is the forest, the big picture, so don't be too effusive and don't get hung up on describing each tree. You can achieve a balance by including good, emotionally informative images in appropriate places, but not so many that your story itself is lost in the descriptions of too many images or mired in images that are extravagant or overstated.

TellTale Soul Pamela uses just the right touch of descriptive imagery while conveying deep attachment and sentiment in a humorous style as she invites readers to travel to the ocean beside her mother and herself.

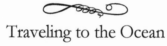

Traveling to the Ocean
~Pamela S. Wight

I am here again, traveling along the same flat road, watching the tall green maples and oaks turn to scrubby, smaller bush and pine. What is it about my primordial need to return to the ocean, the Atlantic Ocean, every summer?

As I breathe in the hot humid New Jersey air, a mixture of dirt, gas, grass, asphalt, and salt water, I wonder if it is just a childhood memory that needs to be rewritten and retold yearly. After all, as a child I crossed the southern hemisphere of New Jersey, traveling from the little town of Pitman to Ocean City at least four or five times a summer. At one hour one-way, that amounted to fifteen hours round trip each summer for eighteen years— two hundred seventy hours of my childhood spent traveling to and from the Atlantic Ocean.

But it is more than that. It is . . .

"Why is he traveling so closely behind you? How fast are you going?" My mother interrupts my slow, careful thoughts.

"I'm going seventy miles per hour," I answer defensively. Actually, the speedometer reads sixty-nine, but I know that will not satisfy her. On this particular trip, we are traveling alone, my seventy-something mother and me, to Ocean City on a gorgeous, sparkling, ninety-three degree Saturday morning. We will arrive at our rented house, two blocks from the beach, eight hours before my brother and his family join us.

"That's too slow," she responds. "The speed limit is sixty-five. I go at least seventy-five."

I allow my eyes to leave the road to give my mom a small smile. She is younger than I in so many ways. Always has been, and I've always been older than she. That's one of the reasons we enjoy each other's company so much.

"You convinced me to let you drive my car," she continues, "so don't give me that look that says I can't be a front seat driver."

I just smile a little wider. We are enjoying ourselves in her little white Chevrolet Le Baron convertible. The top is down; the wind is in our hair. I decide to bite my tongue and not tell her I am driving particularly because she insists on driving eighty miles per hour when the speed limit is sixty-five.

I look in the rear view mirror. A big black sports utility vehicle is barely a foot away from my bumper. I am in the fast lane and can't move over to the right lane because of a string of slower cars.

"Back off," I mumble. I tap my brake lightly, but he doesn't slow down a bit.

"Go faster," my dear mother says. Her short white hair is whipped against her head like a cap. Her tanned legs are crossed comfortably in front of her, showing off light blue short shorts. Her white tank top accentuates tanned, muscled arms. Some people would look at her and think that she plays tennis and lifts weights five days a week. They'd be right.

"Mom, I can't go faster, then I'd be right on the bumper of the person in front of me. Besides, I don't want to go faster." Why do I feel like the prim and proper old aunt?

She sighs and fidgets for four more minutes. Finally, I find an opening in the right hand lane, turn on the blinker, and begin to move over.

"Give 'em the finger," she demands.

Lynn Cook Henriksen

"What? Mom!" I respond in shock.

"Come on, give 'em the finger," my pretty, demure mother, grandmother of four, insists.

No, I won't. I am afraid she is going to make me. At my age, I don't need to give in like I did at six, or sixteen, or even twenty-six. I smooth into the right lane and begin to relax until I see my mother push toward me and lean over my lap. She holds her face up high, as high as her five foot two inch frame allows, and yells to the driver of the car passing us on the left, "J E R K," in a long, loud, reverberating scream. I stare at this woman and then look at the face of the driver as he, too, stares open-mouthed. He looks hurt that this small, cute, but older woman would be chastising him so harshly. As he lifts his arms and hands in supplication, I begin to laugh, first gently so I make no sound, and only my stomach rises quickly in and out; then I release myself and laugh until it hurts.

"Why didn't you give him the finger?" She asks, when I am finished.

"Mom, you are too much," I answer.

Her expression is surprised, like what did I do?

I think of the times our differences used to bother me: she was always short, cute, and feminine; I felt too tall, awkward, big. She was the social one; I was the loner. She was assertive; I stood in the background, watching.

"Love you mom," I say just as a big wheeler passes us noisily on the left. I'm not sure she hears me, but she has a small, secretive smile on her elfin face.

Photo contributed by Pamela: With Mom - Ocean City, NJ

Pamela Wight: "I have traveled to the ocean with my mom for over 50 years. We lived coasts apart for years, and now live four states away, but always get together to share the ocean. I am a creative writing teacher, a wife, and the mother of two incredible children, who now have babies of their own. This past August, all four generations traveled together to the ocean."

Do you feel you came away from reading Pam's story with a good image of her mother's personality? Go back through *Traveling to the Ocean* and mark words, colorful dialogue, or passages that made her mother's spirit come alive for you and take note of how Pam achieved it. Actually, do the same with Lynn Scott's story a few pages back.

> **WRITE** two pages capturing your mother's personality as best you can by looking beneath her exterior persona. For example, what do you see behind her smile, what do you intuit behind her tears—essentially, what makes her tick?

Some of what you picked up in the exercise above regarding your mother's character, you can now add to the draft of your true tale. Your story will move others when you detail the "stuff" of life through COLOR, EMOTION, and CHARACTER. Mixing these elements together also produces interesting results—coloring emotion communicates depth of character. We'll discuss using your imagination in resourceful ways later on in this act.

Add elements in creative layers. Like a painter continuing to stroke the canvas, oil over oil, refining his artistic vision, you will layer your story by adding texturizing strokes of emotion and color to define your mother's key characteristics through words on paper.

Which of the following sentences, first written, then stroked by a *TellTale Soul*, do you find most interesting and creative?
1) *"When she got really angry, all I wanted to do was disappear."*
2) *"Mama's mood turned on a dime, face contorting, tongue flashing a distasteful gray between lips no longer recognizable, I knew it was time to steal away to that place inside myself she couldn't reach."*

Think of adding color figuratively (metaphorically) and literally, as with the use of descriptive words, by adding colorful characterizations that put oomph and vitality into fine points and images. As easy an act as using adjectives to enliven nouns will make your story better, but don't overdo the adjectives, either. In the two previous stories, note that the adjectives—the modifiers of nouns—were not overused by the authors.

As you continue through all five of the acts in this book, you will digest many more elements of what it takes to make your bio-vignette full, strong, and vibrant. You'll learn simply by keeping an open mind, following the exercises and steps I offer, and trusting the process that your story will unfold skillfully.

Your mother's personality will be depicted in a special light by her unique actions, stemming from her very core, when, through your creative writing, you show us who she is. As a collector of stories, I revel in this light; it is this reflection of our mothers that ignites the radiant, prismatic glow making up the spectrum of our collective souls, but we will wait until Act Five to celebrate the universality of the female spirit. For now we'll continue with the art and craft of writing *Mother Memoir*.

Let's look more deeply into conveying emotion through story, and, while we are at it, realize this is the time to stay steadfast in truth and not overwrite our stories in the attempt to gain acceptance or gratuitous compassion. I believe other people can spot insincerity quickly, and it serves no purpose for a *TellTale Soul* to veer away from honesty. We may be tempted to tell it like we think it should be rather than to tell it like it is. This holds true for our individual emotional responses, as well as for the reaction we may look to get from people who read or critique our stories.

CRITIQUEING

Good friends who are not afraid to be constructively honest with you, instructors, editors, or critique groups are good resources for feedback on your work. They are invaluable in uncovering essential items in your story you may have missed because you can't see the forest for the trees—and, to be honest, most writers can't. The following list of questions and elements to look for when requesting feedback or to follow on your own account begins with the words, Have I...

➢ hooked the reader with my opening?
➢ used descriptive imagery and characterization?
➢ set my story in time and place?
➢ linked and clearly shown the essential parts of my bio-vignette, so that a stranger would not be left questioning?
➢ created convincing conflict or tension to make the story compelling?
➢ portrayed my mother's character from the inside out?
➢ presented my mother and myself in the light of truth?
➢ demonstrated a lesson, realization, understanding, or gained wisdom by telling this tale?

The best way to write passion and emotion into your story is to put yourself in your character's shoes. As you're remembering certain moments in time, imagine yourself in each scene with your character. With a little practice, you will learn to use your innate powers of imagination and compassion to feel what the other person is feeling, so that you'll infuse your story with emotional intensity and enthusiastic passion. By envisioning the scenes, you'll come up with ideas and feelings that may not have occurred to you before and, in so doing, create the tone and mood of your story.

TONE AND MOOD

The *tone* of your story is determined by the choices you make in style, relating incidents, or coloring your character. It is the way you sound when telling a story—the set of your *attitude*. It's not what is happening, but how you put across the effect incidents and characters have on you. Tone often refers to voice, and it is a way of conveying the *mood*, the *atmosphere*, the overall feeling or spirit of your story.

Both tone and mood can shift as your story moves from one aspect to the next. For example, the tone you evoke may be gentle, somber, or humorous, whether the mood of your *Mother Memoir* is dark or light. Think of your story as a song in which you could sing the lyrics in many different ways—using an angry voice, a sad voice, or a joyful voice, among others.

> **WRITE** one paragraph describing the tone you
> set for your bio-vignette and another paragraph
> on the overall mood of your story to see if the
> resulting effect conveys your honest point of view
> and true emotions.

As you continue to center on your attitudes toward your mother and the way in which you tell your story, stay alert as to whom your mother is as an individual unto herself. Remember she has the starring role, and you need to convey her emotions as her unique emotions, not yours. The following sentences, taken from the story Karen Coleman wrote in Act One, reiterate a daughter's perception vis-à-vis her mother's emotional reaction as a result of her actions toward her mom:

> *I don't think there was any way at that place in time that
> she could have found her voice. The pain was too great. I
> had embarrassed my mother as only her child could.*

Telling this truth took courage for Karen because she had to look closely at both sides of an emotional conflict between her mother and herself in order to understand what had transpired. An integral part of writing *Mother Memoir* is transferring your mother's feelings to paper after you have stood in her place and emulated how she may have felt in certain circumstances, telling what it was like for her, as well as what it was like for you. Bring her spirit to the forefront, alive with passion and emotion. Imagine how your mother will feel knowing you wanted to get in touch with her innermost feelings. In addition, anyone reading your story can't know what you realized about your mom's emotions and actions if you don't show them. No one can read your mind or know what is in your heart; they can only feel and realize what you bring to life through your written word—so this responsibility is yours alone, and it is a big one.

Now that you know how to get in touch with the emotion and passion of your character to set the scene—write your heart out. Get that raw emotion down on paper. Make us laugh or make us cry, and portray, like never before in writing, the passion you have discovered that will make your voice strong, your story powerful. You needn't be concerned, at this point, about how to open your story or what to add as finishing touches. We will wait until Act Four to go in depth on those particular issues, since you have just begun the work of adding depth, design, and color to your *Mother Memoir*.

You are here, first and foremost, to illuminate the character and spirit of your mother by writing a bio-vignette. However, many of you will include other people in your stories for emotional appeal, to get certain points across, add dimension, or to set scenes deemed necessary in order to tell your story as you want it told. How you cast these extras is the next thing to consider.

Any character you decide to write into your story needs to have a defined role. It's your job to see that your characters do something, rather than merely mentioning them. Ask yourself questions about each one of them: Why is this person in my story? Is this man important to the story? Does the story work better without an appearance from this woman? If you think certain characters are not worth giving even a semi-active role or if they seem to get in the way of the narrative, get rid of them. Everyone needs a reason for being, right? Well, give them that reason for being, or out they go.

Each character, however, doesn't need a balanced role—use or manipulate a character for a desired effect, and don't make excuses for him. For example, you mention your dad in a story you are writing about your mother. For the story to make sense, you need to depict him, let's say, as a jerk, which is only one aspect of his character. Since this story is not about him, it is not necessary or appropriate to show the reader his good side. Bear in mind, when there is a clash between your characters, tension is achieved; this resulting tension will give your story a desirable edge. In addition, when you don't fully describe some of your characters, you leave something to the readers' imagination, often resulting in a more universal appeal. This little bit of mystery gives people the opportunity to read something into the characters—to see them as similar to people they know, including themselves.

Compelling dialogue is another way to allow your characters to interact and to express feelings and emotion. However, in writing *Mother Memoir*, dialogue is perhaps used to best advantage when it is a conversation between your mother and yourself. Dialogue can be tricky to write, but don't hesitate using it—it is powerful. It's a great tool to use to add emotion rather quickly, and it does frame your story in an interesting way more often than not. Write dialogue by imagining a regular conversation between two people. I suggested to you from the beginning to write your bio-vignette as though you were telling someone the story—the same holds true when adding dialogue. Write conversationally. When people talk they generally use short sentences with distinct but unpretentious words in a back-and-forth manner. When you are writing a short piece like your *Mother Memoir*, a few lines of dialogue here and there create an important emotional impact. *TellTale Soul* Helena wrote:

Sweet Persimmons

~Helena Wan

I rang the doorbell and waited, my thoughts going back so many years to the little girl I was, eagerly awaiting the crack of dawn so I could go to the beach outing with my father and mother—one time per year, always on September first. The day had finally arrived. I hadn't slept a wink the night before and I could not wait any longer. The key on the inside clicked, the chain on the top slid away from its slot, the door swung open, pulling me back into the present moment. There, meeting my eager glance, was the smiling face of my aging mother. "Daughter, you are home at last!" she quietly exclaimed.

In all my memories of my mother, she does not smile often; but when she does, it is like watching the peony bloom in my garden. Every intricate petal unfolded, revealing the golden yellow heart, sweet with nectar. When my mother does not smile, her brow knits tightly together in deep furrows. The corners of her mouth droop, as if dragged down by weights. She looks tired, sad and all alone. This image of her haunts me when I am far away, and, with it, the memories of the hardships in her life as wife, mother, and woman. I am also haunted by her laughter, which was even less frequent than her smiles. Her laughter has always lit up my heart like fireworks in the night sky or birthday presents. I wish my mother would laugh more often.

My mother has seen a lot of history-in-the-making in her lifetime. I have often wondered how different my mother's life—and my life, too—would have been had she not gone through those difficult times.

Six years into the new Republic of China in 1911—following the collapse of the Manchu Dynasty, the last to rule China—in the tiny British outpost on the southeastern edge of China on an island called Hong Kong a baby girl was born. This baby was my mother, the forth daughter borne by my grandmother. My grandmother was hoping for a son, no doubt, and her husband said, "Let us name her 'Precious Hope,' and maybe we will have a son next time." Soon enough, the fifth child arrived, a boy in glory when he was born, and "Glory" became his name.

My mother's mother was illiterate—illiteracy was considered a womanly virtue at that time—and very beautiful, which was nearly a detriment to her. A wealthy merchant, admiring her looks, wanted her as his second wife. My mother's mother would become no such thing and chose instead to be the one and only wife of a man with little money. My mother inherited this independence of spirit, for she, too, chose her own life companion when she was ripe for marriage.

The new republic into which my mother was born brought other new values and freedoms as well. My mother banished the old virtue of female illiteracy to the wind and, as if quenching her thirst with cool sparkling water on a hot summer day, she went through her education from elementary to secondary and on to college in one gulp. She became well-versed in the Chinese classics, skilled in poetry writing, and acquired a fine hand in calligraphy. I admired my mother's literary knowledge greatly, like a child idolizing the classmate who played a fine hand of piano on stage in front of the entire school.

My mother's career goal was to be a teacher, and she took a second job at home to be my teacher as soon as I, at three, became educable. She was a very strict teacher. She made me memorize awful passages with archaic words, which held no meaning for me. "These are poems of the Ninth Century Tang Dynasty, and there are three hundred of them that I want you to recite," she said. "Now hold the brush upright and make this downstroke as straight and strong as a bamboo branch." She would strike a blow to my hand or head if I made a wrong move. I became her obedient disciple, at times glad to bask in her attention, other times grudgingly, with tears in my eyes, when she hurt my pride or my hide.

Now I laid down my luggage in my mother's apartment and felt back-to-the-womb safety and comfort in her presence, rendering my adult sense of independence obsolete on this homecoming visit. I surrendered to her nurturing, which comes mostly in the form of food. "Come to the table," she beckoned, "I have made your favorite dish." I took a bite of the delicately flavored minced pork with eggs and crab. It tasted every bit like she used to make it. "But where is the crab?" I asked. My mother laughed her heart-lifting laugh. It suddenly dawned on me that she was pulling an old trick on me. It happened one day long ago that my mother, while making that dish, left out the crab but kept in the garlic, which was what distinguished the dish from its ordinary version made without the crab or the garlic, and we fell for it. We all laughed, I most heartily, second only to my mother's laughter which rang across the room, bounced against the wall and back, like flying boomerang.

Tomorrow she would take me to a Thai buffet; the day after to a dim sum lunch with high tea at the Mandarin hotel. My mother had already worked out each and every meal I was going to eat during my two-week visit *with her. I watched myself in my mind's mirror grow ten pounds heavier, bulging in all the wrong places.*

But first, she wanted to know if I would accompany her to the market in the morning, thinking I might want to share in her passion. Going to the market is a ritual that follows well mapped-out plans. First she would tour all the open-air vegetable stalls, noting and comparing prices, then on to the covered market to scrutinize the fish and the meat. Only on the second round would she make her purchases. I have often wondered, following her from stall to stall, how she could possibly tell minute differences in quality or remember all those prices without having to jot them down. My mother loves food and she loves bargains. She is frugality personified. It is also her way to show one-upmanship. I remember an exchange between her and my father:

Mother: "How much are those grapes?"

Father: "How much do you think?"

Mother: "I wouldn't pay more than 30 cents a bunch."

Father: "Guess what? That was exactly how much I paid."

Mother: "In fact, I saw some of even better quality than these yesterday, and they were only 25 cents a bunch!"

One-upmanship or not, my mother managed to keep her family with two young children alive during the war with the Japanese, while so many others died of starvation. Whatever was edible my mother gave to me, since I was her first-born, then to my sister, then to my father, and to herself last, if there was anything left.

She walked the many miles to the school where she taught, rather than spending the one-penny fare. She walked until holes appeared in the soles of her only pair of shoes. My mother had healthy, rounded cheeks when she was a young girl, but by the war's end she was reduced to mere bones and skin. Her eyes had developed a sad, haunted look, and her body was riddled with illness brought on by years of malnutrition.

It was ten years before she felt strong enough to bear more children. Then my mother had two more daughters and, just like her mother before her, she finally had a son, whom she named simply "Joy." At last her life was complete. Almost.

Years of deprivation and war had left our family quarters badly in need of repair. The crickety, long, dark wooden stairs up to the top floor where we lived haunted my mother's every step. The roof leaked in many places and the termites nested. Worse than the water coming in were those termites when they decided to migrate; they rained down on us in droves in the stealth of darkness, putting an end to our sleep for the night. And we looked to Mother to save us from all this—my father was at work dawn till dark.

Left alone, my mother had to decide for us all. She would have to amass enough money for a new apartment with her limited resources and seven mouths to feed. She could not stand the thought of her family in danger— trapped under rubble should that old building collapse or engulfed by flames if the wooden structure caught fire. She had to look for a safe haven for her children. She worked toward that goal with feverish earnestness and haste. Our life was stripped to the barest necessities: meals with lots of beans and very little meat, no new clothes, no telephone or radio. We wore our school uniforms inside and outside school, living like ascetics in a cut-off world. I waited patiently, helping whenever I could.

The day came when my mother said to me, "There is an apartment in a newly built building that I am going to buy." We all went to look at it. It was on the fifth floor—not the top, thank heaven—so no fear of leaky roof. The solid walls were fireproof concrete. Best of all were those modern amenities we had only dreamed of: a gas stove for cooking, modern flush toilets, shiny smooth hardwood floors. No more begging to use the neighbor's telephone. We could have a radio to listen to sweet Doris Day or trembling Elvis Presley. How exciting it would be to make ice, mold gelatin, and prevent ice cream from melting! My mother would no longer have to labor for hours over the washboard to clean our clothes. And to top it all, there would be air-conditioning to stave off the oppressive summer heat and a television to watch all the movies we wanted. All in our own home?

Praise to our mother, who led us out of the darkness into the brave new Sputnik age! We shed our old life like a snake sheds its skin and slipped away without ever a glance back. It was our family's Great Leap forward. And then, despite the hard times, she eventually put all of her children through college. How did she do it?

And now 35 years later it is June 1997, and I have only four more days to stay with her. Like a little girl, I entreated my mother to tell me the stories of long ago. She is a great storyteller, and over the years her skill has not diminished, but like a tumbling stone in the stream it becomes polished like a smooth round pebble. She has the ability to tell the same story again and again as though she has never told it before. And each time it was new to my ear. I begged my mother to write down all her stories. But I thought, without the voice behind them, they would be mere words on paper, still and without spirit, like exhausted butterflies at summer's end.

Then my mother handed me a bunch of poems she had written recently. Her calligraphy is as fine as ever, full of elegant strokes, energy, and grace. Most of the poetry is poignant, though there are some cheerful and courageous verses. They let me peer into the window of my mother's soul, and I see a woman of profound depth of feelings—of pride, perseverance, loyalty, resilience, courage, and self-sacrifice. (I felt I was so much more selfish and intolerant compared with my mother.) I also saw her vulnerability, her insecurities, her sadness, her loneliness paired with the simplicity and tranquility that comes with old age. How odd it seemed to me for my mother to have a youthful and active mind trapped in an aged body. May my mother's heart stay forever young!

With my mother's poems packed safely away in my luggage, I bade her farewell. "Promise to come back soon!" my mother said.

"I shall see you first in California this fall," I reminded her.

"It is getting harder and harder for me to travel these days. Come back when the weather is cooler," she insisted.

"The sweet persimmons will be in season in San Francisco in November, waiting for you!" I shouted before the elevator swallowed me, my mother's words still ringing in my ears.

"My daughter, there will not be many more years for me to see you again. So come back soon!"

I will, Mother. I promise.

Although I don't have Helena's photo or personal remarks to share with you, her story was one of the first treasures in my collection. I admire her beautiful writing style, compassion, and depth of understanding. Her *Mother Memoir* is longer than most, because she felt every word of it was necessary to make the *one* story she wanted to write complete. I find it encompasses the passion and mindfulness crafted through deft character portrayals and just the right mix of humorous and poignant dialogue that *TellTale Souls* seek.

As we leave this section there is a question I would like you to answer, not by writing, but through careful thought. Ask yourself if there is something you have left out, overlooked, or buried that would make your story convey even greater emotion and passion.

Whether it is your story that you're working on, writing, rereading, and writing some more, or whether it is someone else's story you've read, it is important to pause and reflect mindfully on what has been revealed. Make conscious connections. Ask yourself how this makes you feel, and why? Throughout the years working with *TellTale Souls*, I know how earnest writers feel about the stories they have written. The messages they communicate have come from deep within their hearts and souls. They expose the most intimate and heartfelt areas of their lives. Now you're following their lead. Step lightly, with compassion and humility for all.

TRIGGERING CREATIVITY AND EMBRACING SIMPLICITY

There are thousands of words, phrases, and just bits and pieces of things that float in and out of our consciousness that have a way of shaking up memories of our mothers. Sometimes they give us a start, and we actually spend time thinking about mom, other times we simply cannot be bothered. We shrug and think we'll return to that thought later, when we have *time*...but more than likely we don't return. But now you're here, so it is a good bet you are in the mood to make time for what you feel is important work.

The ideas we glean from what I call "character signals" are the sparks we need to add the rich details that put depth into our stories. I made a list of these signals for you below, but you'll think of many more on your own. As you go through the words and examples (excerpts from stories by *TellTale Souls*) I've included, fleeting thoughts, images, ideas, impressions, and emotions will surface in your mind. Take time with each word and write as you go; jot a word or two on a piece of paper so that these nuggets, these gems of emerging ideas, won't slip away. You will want to expand upon your notes later when you're working on your story.

Character Signals:

> ➤ **Songs**
>
>   *My mother's beautiful alto voice rose and fell softly, filtering through the walls of the house. "You are my sunshine, my only sunshine. You*

make me happy when skies are gray. You'll never know, dear, how much I love you . . ."

➤ **Clothing**

Are you kidding? You can't wear that outfit to come to my school.

➤ **Rooms** — Search each one for clues.

My mother believed in allowing us the space to be creative . . . we drew masterpieces on our kitchen table and covered our bedroom walls with murals.

➤ **Perfumes**

. . . and when I close my eyes I can still smell her signature perfume.

➤ **Weather**

. . . it was pouring rain and windy. Mama was wet to the skin and brimming with urgency, one hand holding down her navy blue hat, she pulled her billowing blue cape close around her bulging abdomen, stepped into the street, and, as luck would have it, managed to wave down a fellow driving a pick-up truck.

➤ **Furniture**

. . . rearranging it seemed a favorite hobby.

➤ **Colors**

Have you ever been forced to eat blue mashed potatoes?

➤ **Hobbies** — Peculiar ones can be the most fun.

Aunt Liz collected recipes of all kinds for the fifty years I knew her, but never cooked a day in her life.

➤ **Habits** — Compulsive ones can be irritating.

She searched the paper daily and went to every garage sale she could find for miles around and couldn't pass by a yard sale anytime she was driving down the road, even if it made her late for an appointment.

➤ **Rituals**

. . . my mom would cuddle in bed with me each night for about half an hour of reading. Then she'd silently wait until I was fast asleep so she could finally sneak out of my room, hoping I wouldn't wake

up. I called this "read me to bed," which shortened over the years to just "read me."

> ## Traditions
My dad thought his way was the only way to carve the Thanksgiving turkey. Well, he thought wrong.

> ## Scents & Smells
The odors of Hilex bleach, cooking, and wash water blended into one familiar and comforting smell.

> ## Voices or Accents
In a silent, "inside" connection with my mother, I says, "Mama, how do I make a sleeve, an armhole?" She looks me square in my mind's eye and guides me with the best advice I've ever had, "Well, ya jes looks at it, Baby Rose, and ya jes draws it and ya jes do it."

> ## Colloquialisms
Now just cause you got some schoolin', don't you be gettin' 'bove ya'lls raisin'.

> ## Foods
And love. Love was your favorite pie made as a surprise when you least deserved it; any breakfast you wanted before you ventured out to walk the three blocks to school on cold, blustery winter mornings; home-made syrups and jellies from wild berries and fruits she picked and preserved; cream pudding you could eat before dinner; stuffed chickens on Sundays.

> ## Movies/Plays
When Jaws leapt out the first time on the screen, it scared her so badly she drenched the man in front of her with Coca Cola.

> ## Prayers
God loves every rock and tree and so does he love thee.

> ## Lessons
You will see that all I have been trying to teach you is already within you. I am just trying to give you words to describe what is in your heart.

➤ **Recipes**

To begin with, Mom made a complicated grilled cheese sandwich. She toasted the bread separately, chopped up cheese and onions and melted them together in a cast iron skillet and then spread the sticky mixture on the toast.

➤ **Games**

He tried to get me to play chess, I didn't like board games. Why couldn't he see Kick-the-Can was more fun for me? She could see it, but that didn't count.

➤ **Books**

She never met a book she didn't like.

➤ **Relationships**

More than once, when she did speak of her own early childhood, she spoke of her father's skill and gift with the violin and of her mother's gentle, but frail beauty and of their devotion to each other. She spoke of inheriting neither. But I suspected that she had come to refer to herself as Grandpa saw her and not as she truly was.

➤ **Vacations**

We'd all five of us, with luggage, lunch, and all, be packed into the car ready to go on our yearly one-week vacation, when Dad would decide he needed to change the oil before driving off—he did this more than once. Mom never said a word.

➤ **Seashore/Mountains**

Mom loved spacing out at the seashore so much, she often forgot she had children wading out too far in the surf.

➤ **Jewelry**

You mean you actually gave Grandma Jenny's jewelry to the thrift shop?

➤ **Animals/Pets**

This farm was my magic kingdom...the main characters were the mischievous animals, aptly named by Grandma Samantha.

➤ **Motherisms**

Mom said, "Put on a sweater child, I'm cold."

What did any of these ideas conjure up for you? It can be a lot of fun discussing the triggers that excited or inspired you. Make connections. Talk to others.

WRITE: Incorporate some of the ideas that were spawned by this exercise into your short, true tale.

Now that creative new ideas have been generated by the prompts above, let's look at embracing simplicity as you write. Simplicity in writing doesn't mean it is simple or particularly easy to do, and it does not mean getting your thoughts down on paper and making sense of key memories isn't complicated. Writers work hard at their craft day in and day out. But don't let hard work discourage you or get in your way as you venture into memoir, because writing memoir is one of the most meaningful things you will ever accomplish. Ban spirit dampening thoughts.

What you will achieve, through tapping memory, is writing a story detailing your truths clearly by telling it as you see it in a straightforward, interesting style. By making the most of your passion and staking claim to this telling tale, you will be stimulated to add unusual bits and memory morsels that will illuminate the character of your mother in a way unique to her and to your story.

Simplicity is the key to clear writing and better reading. Aim for it. You can cut out unnecessary words and rewrite unclear sentences. You may, at first, think adding more words or composing complicated sentences will make your story sound more important. It has the opposite effect on the story. Unnecessary words and complex or poor structure clutter your work and take away from its clarity and strength. Don't make the reader work hard to get your meaning or be turned off by the use of superfluous verbiage. If the reader gets lost, that means you haven't done your job as a writer clearly enough. We read stories for a variety of reasons—fun, relaxation, adventure, connection, fulfillment, and emotional stimulation—in a word, enjoyment.

Look closely at your sentences as you ask yourself these questions:

> ➤ Are there words I can forego and still get my meaning across?
> ➤ Could a shorter, simpler word replace a long word?
> ➤ Are my compound or complex sentences distracting?
> ➤ Does the subject match the predicate?
> ➤ Have I duplicated adjectives?
> ➤ Have I used adverbs that weaken the verb?
> ➤ Am I watching my tenses (past, present, and future)?
> ➤ Am I maintaining consistent use of pronouns?
> ➤ Are my paragraphs too long? Readers need space.

There are simile and metaphor, paradox, alliteration, symbol, irony, hyperbole, onomatopoeia, and other interesting literary devices to use in your writing. And, when they're used well, they are wonderful additions, but when they are not, they detract from a story. I have placed a glossary of literary terms and devices for *TellTale Souls* at the end of this guide for your reference.

I mentioned earlier that the addition of adjectives often enhances your work, but look closely at the choice of adjectives you used to modify nouns. Often, simply substituting one adjective for another or getting rid of it altogether makes a statement more powerful. Also check to see if your sentence would be stronger if you reversed its structure. This reversal technique works for paragraphs, too.

WRITE, REWRITE: As you write, continually ask yourself if the sentence or paragraph you wrote makes sense—are your thoughts clearly stated? Repeat this exercise throughout your story and rework it, and then ask yourself if the sentences and paragraphs follow each other logically.

The final self-test is to read your work aloud as though you have never heard it before, as through the eyes and ears of a stranger. Would that person find your story easy to follow and laid out clearly? If you have any doubts, work your trouble spots until they are no longer troubling or throw them out altogether. But before blotting them into oblivion, let your story sit. Give it and yourself a break and come back to it when you are refreshed. A troublesome passage is often easy to fix after giving yourself some distance from it. People vary by how much time they need to come back to a piece of writing and see it more clearly. I recommend waiting overnight, at the very least.

FOCUSING YOUR POWER

From your practice so far in directing your powers of concentration inward and discovering fresh meaning in old memories and in newly found images, you are living proof of the power of focus. You have realized how to:

> ➤ Let mental pictures converge with feeling and emotion.
> ➤ Keep certain memories the center of interest.
> ➤ Render images with definition and clarity.

You have discovered the theme or premise of the story that captures the character and spirit of your mother—so keep your eye on the prize. Focus your power by holding fast to just those images and ideas that you want recorded in your memoir. Keep in mind the idea of parameters—the framework whereby your story needs to be contained so your story won't get out of control. Now, on to the next step in containing your focus powerfully: You must focus on how you write at the same time as you stay on track with the premise of your bio-vignette. It's time to look at how to narrow your writing focus, so you write to get your points across without injecting unnecessary information that will result in crushing your work with material extraneous to the story itself.

Only you can determine which details are significant to your story. Think about what you want to express about your mother to make her character commanding, as the basic idea for your story remains a vibrant focus. If your story takes unexpected turns that open your eyes to new vistas or facets, which it is likely to do as it progresses, and you enjoy this new view and feel it adds to the storyline, incorporate it into your writing. But if you stray too far from your original idea, consider pulling the focus back in line with what you want told. Don't give up your power by adding features which may do nothing more than confuse.

Blair Kilpatrick recently added her *Mother Memoir* to my *TellTale Souls* collection. She covers a lot of ground in the telling of her tale, while staying focused on the premise—the family her mother-in-law unwittingly provided.

Gifts from My Mother-in-Law
~Blair Kilpatrick

My mother-in-law and I didn't get off to the most promising start.

When my boyfriend took me to New York to meet his family, I already had one big strike against me: I wasn't Jewish.

We hadn't told his parents we were thinking about getting married. We certainly didn't tell them it might even happen that summer, a year before we graduated from college.

A pretty, dark-haired woman greeted us at the door. She didn't look old enough to be the mother of a college student. She seemed more like a perky teenager who blurts out the first thing that enters her head.

Here's what popped out, just after our first hello:

"So, do you have a problem with your weight?"

"Well, uh, yes. I guess so."

What else could I say? I'd been dieting on and off since I was eleven, with mixed results. Nice of her to notice.

Maybe she just wanted to bond around diet tips. But—unlike me— this slender woman didn't look like she needed to worry about what she ate.

It took months for the full impact of that outrageous welcome to sink in. Did she mean to be critical? Did she feel competitive? Was she trying to be helpful, in an intrusive kind of way? Or was it simply a case of poor boundaries?

Probably all of those things.

Only now, as I write this, does the other truth, the most important one, hit me: She must have decided, in that moment, that I was already family. Only a mother could get away with a remark like that.

And only a daughter would shrug it off—and still remember it, almost four decades later.

~~~

At first, we thought my husband's parents might not come to Chicago for our wedding. But they showed up—along with both sets of grandparents and a fair number of aunts and uncles, plus a cousin or two. My parents' back yard filled up with family and friends. And, miracle of miracles, everyone got along.

Later that summer, my new in-laws held a reception in New York for the rest of their family who couldn't make it to Chicago. I met dozens more aunts, uncles, cousins. More relatives than I could possibly keep track of. My idea of family opened up, expanded. And I realized that I'd become a part of it. Despite their doubts about mixed marriage—a first for their family—I had been welcomed into the fold.

Especially by my mother-in-law. She made it clear: she'd had three sons and now she had a daughter. Me. In a few years, she'd have one more daughter, when my husband's younger brother got married. Eventually, she'd have a granddaughter, along with three grandsons.

Over the years, my mother-in-law has remained girlish, upbeat, and naïve in her enthusiasms. She doesn't see the shades of grey. She can be prone to quick judgments, sometimes harsh ones. But she is fierce in her attachments, generous to a fault, and extravagant in her praise for those she loves.

She loves giving gifts. I've received beautiful jewelry. Perfume. Hand knit scarves. And a certain amount of clothing that's not to my taste: too tight, impossibly girly, full of ruffles, designed to flaunt my minimal cleavage. I just smile and set it aside.

She is famous for her chocolate chip cookies. She likes to bake them in big batches and mail them to her children and grandchildren. She never did get the hang of packaging. She would send her cookies off in taped up oatmeal canisters, shoeboxes, bulging plastic containers. They would arrive as tasty crumbs. But no one minded.

She's been through some tough times. A divorce. A stretch as a single woman in Manhattan, when she lived in a studio apartment and baked her chocolate chip cookies in a toaster oven. Remarriage to a good man and a new life in Florida. The death of one of her children. The challenge of her second husband's health problems—and then her own. But she's never lost the girlish enthusiasm and the dazzling smile.

When I became a first-time author last year, she was so proud—as though her own child had written a book. Even before my Cajun music memoir came out, she started to scout out local bookstores and talk it up. When I sent her an advance copy of Accordion Dreams, *she started to carry it with her. Just to encourage sales, she said. I joked that I'd have to ask my publisher to make her our official publicist.*

She turned eighty last spring. Her husband organized a celebration: a dinner for her family and close friends. We arranged to fly in for the weekend.

Then my mother-in-law had a brainstorm: why not combine her birthday celebration with a book launch event? She knew I'd been doing readings in California and a few places in the South.

At first, I said no. We would only be there for the weekend. I didn't want to waste half a day on book promotion. This was her celebration, not mine. I was embarrassed at the thought: doing a reading—and playing music—in front of my husband's family, on a day meant to honor my mother-in-law.

But she remained insistent. She knew the perfect bookstore. She would organize it. It was her birthday, wasn't it? This was what she wanted. How could I refuse her?

Finally, I got it. She really wanted to do this. It wasn't just about me.

So we arrived in Florida late on a Friday night. Early Saturday afternoon, we drove to a local bookstore. My mother-in-law laid out a spread of homemade cookies. I talked about my book and read a few passages. Then we played music—me on the Cajun accordion, my husband on the fiddle. We had a good turnout—more than just friends and relatives. It was one of the most attentive audiences I've had at a reading.

Through it all, my mother-in-law beamed. I like to think we gave her naches. It's a Yiddish term that means pride and joy in a child's accomplishment.

That night, we celebrated her birthday. Finally, it was her turn to be in the spotlight.

I'd picked out a pin to give her: A delicate, filigreed tree of silver and little seed pearls. It was the Tree of Life, I told her. But I'm not sure she heard me. She seemed distracted. Far away.

~~~

A few months later, my mother-in-law started to go downhill. She had a series of physical setbacks. Memory lapses. Periods of confusion. She knew something was wrong. She gave away her stock of chocolate chips. She couldn't follow recipes any more, she admitted. She had several hospitalizations.

Finally, a diagnosis: She had early stage Alzheimer's.

~~~

My mother-in law tries to be upbeat about her diagnosis. It could be worse. Lots of people have Alzheimer's, right? She laughs a lot. She is writing down her memories. "My book," she calls it.

When we speak by phone, she often talks about the past. Sometimes she tries to apologize for having been judgmental. For giving me a hard time, when we first met. That's years ago, I tell her. It's all in the past. You have no need to apologize. But when people have dementia, an event from forty years ago can be more vivid than this morning's breakfast. So it's hard for her to let go of the past.

She and her husband have finally moved into an assisted living facility. The condo where they lived for twenty years is up for sale, and they need to get rid of some of their possessions.

Recently, she called about that. She wanted to make sure my husband and I took anything we might want, before the rest got sold. She wanted us to have something of hers, to remember her. Could she set something aside for us? Maybe we'd like the piano.

I assured her we didn't need furniture. We didn't need things at all. I reminded her that I already had two beautiful old European rings she had passed on to me, many years ago. One had had been her mother's, the other a gift from my husband's father.

Yes, she remembered now. She was happy to be reminded about the rings.

Then she recalled something else.

"Didn't I give you a necklace?"

I knew exactly what she meant. I'd been thinking about it myself, but I wasn't sure she'd recall it, because the gift had been a more recent one.

Five years earlier, when we'd flown to Florida to celebrate her seventy-fifth birthday, she'd had three matching gold necklaces made by a local jeweler: one for me, one for my sister-in-law, and one for herself. Each held a personalized gold pendant.

Mine had a lacy "B" at the center of a golden circle. The circle held three tiny birthstones: a garnet for me, an amethyst for my older son, and a ruby for my younger son.

My husband had a place on his own mother's pendant, along with his two brothers. He was the amethyst.

My mother-in-law remembered those necklaces. "I did do that, didn't I? Do you still have yours?"

"Of course I still have it. I wear it on special occasions. It's beautiful."

I wish I had added this:

"The necklace helps me remember: From you, I've developed a deeper understanding of family. And you've given me the best gift of all. My husband and my sons. Without you, I wouldn't have them."

Photo contributed by Blair: Blair dreaming.

Blair Kilpatrick: "I am the author of *Accordion Dreams*, a Cajun-Creole music memoir published in 2009 by the University Press of Mississippi and working on a new book about my mother's Slovenian immigrant roots. When I'm not writing, I work as a psychologist and play the accordion with San Francisco Bay Area band *Sauce Piquante*."

WRITE one page listing and remarking upon the insights you have already become aware of by writing your *Mother Memoir*.

It also takes focus to consciously look at what you have learned from writing your telling tale, because the impact of it is comprised of complex feelings and emotions that take some sorting out. By bringing together the act of writing with the psychological reaction you are experiencing, you may not immediately find the answers you are seeking. You may feel blocked by thinking too hard or by how to coherently express what you want to say in writing. Occasionally, we all experience power failure—at least a little brown-out. If you have come to an unproductive place, try any or all of the following to clear your head and restore your vigor:

- Go for a walk or to the gym.
- Use the *innersearch* exercises in Act Two/Taking Yourself Back in Time.
- Listen to music.
- Read a novel or the news.
- Surf the internet.
- Take a drive in the country.
- Eat a meal.
- Take a nap.
- Try raking rocks—a practice in Zen.

I can get blocked when it comes to washing the dishes or designing a new Excel chart—why should writing be any different? I invariably find that the longer I dwell on how much I don't want to do the task, the more horrific the mere thought of it becomes. On the other hand, if I direct myself to just get started with the process, before I know it the dishes are done, the chart is charted, or I'm knee deep in words. Try it!

There may be times when you throw up your hands and feel you are unworthy to write this bio-vignette. *Who do I think I am, writing a story? Especially this story.* And you say, "I don't have what it takes, the words won't come, my story won't sizzle. I don't know how to make the changes in my story that I know should be made."

"Nonsense," I answer. What's more, I guarantee that once you back off a bit, relax, and revisit those hard to reach, dusty corners of the mind, filled with memories complete with heartfelt passion and emotion, you will burn with the desire to get back to writing. Taking a breather and returning to your writing with renewed energy is exactly what will make your story sizzle.

Try not to be hard on yourself if you falter. In case you didn't know it, you are your toughest critic. Pick up your pencil, dust off your self-esteem, and plug yourself back into the power circuit. By asking yourself the few questions I have listed below, I believe you will set yourself right. Have faith in yourself while thoughtfully answering the following questions:

➢ Do my friends enjoy hearing from me, gossiping or philosophizing with me?
➢ Do I like my way of seeing the world around me?
➢ Are my views on politics, religion, or what to eat for dinner worthwhile?
➢ Do I like my brand of sarcasm, sense of humor, my way of feeling?
➢ Do I want to be heard and listened to?
➢ Do I *deserve* to be heard and listened to?

I hope you answered yes to most, if not all, of those questions. If you answered yes to even one, run with it . . . your unique voice is waiting to be heard. Take a few minutes now to think about the quality, tone, and power of your voice. You are the authority, so to speak, on the story you want remembered about your mother, and you set the tone and mood as you feel it. Now search inwardly with authority to meld your belief in yourself with the memories of your mother to make your story what you direct it to be:

➢ Garner your mental resources.
➢ Take slow, deep breaths, feeling the pleasure of each inhale and each exhale.
➢ Consciously relax each part of your body from your head to your toes.

> ➤ Let the subject of your tale take up your entire consciousness.
> ➤ Travel deeply into the story.
> ➤ Steep in the memories.
> ➤ Relive the events you are remembering, if you feel it is safe to do so.

WRITE a stream of consciousness with whatever thoughts and ideas come to mind. Focus on your mother, and let your words flow until you run out of steam and have several good ideas written down that you can use as the basis for your story or to develop your mother's character.

A gentle reminder of why you are here—*to write the one story that will convey the essence of your mother's character and spirit in the way you want her remembered.* You've learned about confining your story to *one* particular memory or set of interplaying memories that form the foundation of your short, true tale. It's up to you to decide how long a span of time and how many layers you need to make that one main point of your *Mother Memoir.*

I suggest *TellTale Souls* write bio-vignettes that range in length from a page to several pages—you be the judge whether to use more or fewer words. The feedback I've received from both writers and readers boils down to this: Some people get the most out of tightly confined stories revolving around a particular incident, while others enjoy stories spanning a more extended period of the character's life.

The following are three of the shortest stories in the *TellTale Souls* collection, and you have already read the longest true tale, *Sweet Persimmons,* written by Helena Wan in Act Three. Anissa, several years ago at the tender age of nine, wrote the shortest *Mother Memoir* of them all, and she succeeded in capturing her mother's character, as well as her own promising personality. I won't let slip how old the other writers are at this printing, but, since they are adults their personal remarks and photos are included under their succinct, but revealing stories.

Promise Keeper
~Anissa Hamdon-Morison

I like the band called the Indigo Girls. My mom said if they came to Edmonton, she would take me to see them. The day came when the Indigo Girls would be in Calgary, which is "close enough," she said. But, unfortunately, she was going to Lebanon with my dad to help children who live in refugee camps. So she bought three tickets to the Indigo Girls and arranged for me to travel to Calgary with one of my aunts, and then we'd stay at my other aunt's home.

My mother keeps her promises. And she has taught me to behave. I am glad she has taught me to behave, because if none of us knew how to behave, we would have to replace houses with jail cells.

My Hellen
~Mary Anne Coney

Hellen. I don't remember a time when she wasn't with us. She was there before I was four. I know this because she caught me peeking at the birthday cake she'd baked for my fourth birthday party.

Now I am fifty-six, and the one thing I can say about Hellen is that she has always been there for me, as I have for her, and that will be true until one of us draws her last breath.

When I fell down in grade school and sliced open my leg, Hellen was at home to patch me up and make it better. When I had the flu every March,

Hellen made the chicken noodle soup. When Hellen was out of Camel smokes, I went to the little store and bought them for eleven cents a pack. She put up with my pets, she taught me to iron, and she tried to teach me to cook, although that didn't take very well.

She's been "my Hellen" all of my life.

Last year she was in the hospital and nearly died. I was notified and went rushing to be with her. The wardens of the intensive care unit stood in my way. They let me know that only family was permitted inside. I let them know that she was my mother. She's black, I'm white, but they believed me.

As I sat in her room and watched her on the respirator, I could not imagine life without her. She didn't die. Soon she recognized me every visit and tears slid down both of our cheeks because she knew I was there for her as she has always been for me. We didn't have to talk. We just knew.

She's fine now, and we go on like we always have.

Photo contributed by Mary Anne: My Hellen

Mary Anne Coney: "Selecting someone to write about was a challenge. I suppose it seems strange that I chose our housekeep/cook rather than my mother. But Hellen was so much more than that. She was always a mainstay for me no matter what was going on at home."

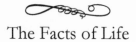

The Facts of Life

~Ann Seymour

I learned the facts of life one day when Mom gave me a book on how chickens reproduced, and it seemed to jibe with what Susan Adams across the street had said. I didn't intend to have anything to do with such practices.

When I handed her back the book, Mom said, "Fine. Then you've finished it. Now I'll give you a new book on King Arthur that a friend in the White Boar Society gave me."

She belonged to this London-based society dedicated to proving that one of the English Kings did not lock his nephews in the tower. Someone else did it, they claim, but I forget who.

The thick book didn't look too tempting, so I asked her to tell me a little bit about the king herself. After explaining that she hadn't actually read that book yet, she began a recitation of him and his era in England, adding historic perspective on the context of his life. It took over an hour, but she finished with, "Of course, these are just a few highlights."

Photo contributed by Ann: Ann with a knowing look in her eye.

Lynn Cook Henriksen

Ann Seymour: "I studied under Wallace Stegner at Stanford and became a journalist, much to Mom's horror. She's the you-never-allow-your-name-in-the-paper generation. Writing on the Internet's fine, as she doesn't think it really exists, at least not in a meaningful form for the centogenarian set." Seymour is the author of *I've Always Loved You: A True Story of WW II in California, the Pacific battlefields, and the Imperial Palace in Japan.*

CENTERING WITH TRUTH, IMAGINATION, AND INTUITION

Memoir can be exquisitely revealing. When you tell the truths that must be told in order to create a credible story, your soul lies unadorned before your readers' eyes. You want to write your story with all honesty, but you may also feel bending the truth will help fulfill your need for personal acceptance and acknowledgment as a writer. Don't compromise the truth for acceptance. The conflict over truth that you may encounter from the onset is a good thing, actually. Conflict creates tension. Tension is exactly what will keep you thoroughly involved in your writing.

I support your using imagination in resourceful ways. Nevertheless, always tell the truth, as you see it, and be clear and transparent in doing so. Imagination in nonfiction, as I see it, doesn't mean making things up, and it occupies a significant place when used towards honest ends. It means opening things up, making them richer by bringing elements into the picture that are true to form for your character, but may not have happened at the exact moment in time in which your story is set.

When you want your writing to really work well, it must ring true to your ears and to your readers' minds. Therefore, don't hold material elements back. Tell the whole truth, not just part of it. You have to dig deep for the well to run clean; the seepage of untruths will sour the water. Fabrications are the stuff of novels, not memoir. Truth and clarity go hand in hand, because simplicity and transparency clear the way for the truth to be told.

You're telling a true story. Yet, to get your ideas and feelings across with impact, facts and events may require enhancement. Another way to think of this is to remember that memories can play tricks on you and, in return, you can play around with memories just a little by fluffing them up. As an example, you recall your mother's cat, Fluffy, was always at her feet while she knitted in the evenings, but you are not positive Fluffy was actually there the evening she threw the sweater she was knitting for your father into the fire. It's okay to set your scene with Fluffy at her feet.

Think of it this way, through actively engaging your imagination you are getting to the heart of your character—what makes her tick, what incites passion in her—not just what's on the surface at particular moments. Dig into the inner workings of her character. To make certain story points carry more weight, your use of items that and beings who provoke emotional reactions from her are necessary to include. In addition, and to gain insight and understanding, look for the reasons why something is causing a psychological pull on her. You set the tone of your story by injecting passion and emotion as you see it in others and as you feel it—engage your imagination.

Truth can be factual or you can uncover it through emotional memory which is the most powerful way to add passion to your bio-vignette. We all have emotional memory, and it is best illuminated through the power of imagination when recalling the emotions we felt at the time an incident occurred. The best way to write passion and emotion into your story is to place yourself in mama's shoes—as comfortable or uncomfortable as that may be.

First choose a highly impactful memory involving emotional interaction between your mother and yourself—one where passion is palpable. (This doesn't need to be a memory from the story you are writing—this is a practice designed to get you working with emotional memory.) Then, **WRITE** two paragraphs describing the emotional details that heightened you senses and how you used them to enter into this significant incident. Next, stand in your mother's shoes and write two more paragraphs from her vantage point. By bringing the passion you find within her together with your own passion, greater truths can be realized. Now that you have experienced the power of emotional memory, use this technique to intensify the passion in your *Mother Memoir.*

Go to a quiet place now, close your eyes, let your mind drift to one particular scene that particularly aroused your passion in the exercise above. Draw on all of your senses during this reflection time, because you will create mood from passion by recreating the memory using all of your senses—sight, touch, smell, hearing, taste. We'll work even more with our senses in Act Four, but for the present time realize you can still taste the frosting on your seventh birthday cake before she angrily threw it in the sink; smell the heavenly sent of freshly mown grass in your backyard; listen once again to the melody she often hummed; feel the touch of her hand caressing your cheek; you can even see her face change before your eyes when you bring to life, through your imagination, the time she became furious or saddened by someone she perceived did her wrong.

I remember being frightened as a child when I found my mother sitting in the hallway near the coat closet, back against the wall. Her head was down, both hands cradling her face, shoulders shaking as she sobbed. Mom felt my presence and looked up at me through a blue-gray blur. I said, "Mommy." She managed, "Go outside and play, honey." This unhappy picture flashed in memory many times over the years, not frightening

EMOTIONAL MEMORY

Emotional memory is enhanced memory, heightened by an association between an incident and intense feelings about the event and/or the individuals involved in the experience. Think of it as a process whereby emotional stimuli render some memories more psychologically valuable than others due to the fact they carry a greater electrical charge at the time the memory embedded itself in your brain.

It's literally the stuff you cannot see, and it is essential when you are trying to feel what someone else is feeling. You get there by remembering a similar response in yourself and transferring those emotions to someone else in a comparable situation. In the second place, you can use emotional memory to revisit times and places you wish to more clearly remember by using *innersearch* techniques.

any longer, but it made me sad each time. It wasn't until I took the scene inside myself, determined to find a more complete sense of the incident, that I was able to remember what transpired shortly thereafter: I'd gone out to play, as she asked me to do, but I was worried, so I ever so carefully opened the screen door to the kitchen and crept silently back into the house only to find Mommy talking on the telephone with her mother. I learned, from eavesdropping on her side of the conversation, that she had frantically searched every jacket and coat pocket, every boot and shoe in the closet for a missing twenty dollar bill. This happened at a time when twenty dollars bought groceries for a week. Daddy had pulled anchor and left us for another woman, so my mother worked at our small town butcher shop for meager wages and two pounds of hamburger a week; once in awhile the butcher would throw in enough fish for a meal for four. I also remember hearing my mom laughing so hard she wet her pants. That is a story for another time. But after recreating the missing twenty ordeal, I remembered an honest to goodness fish story that would form the basis for my telling tale.

Cheeks

~Lynn Henriksen

In our family it seemed normal, so I didn't think much about it growing up. Oh yes, I thought it was something special, because we didn't often have it, but it was normal just the same. Didn't every family in our small town enjoy this delicacy?

On those particular evenings, Rickey, Dana, and I would draw in close around our gray-flecked, red-Formica-topped kitchen table, its naive, gently curving, chrome-plated legs holding our weight as our elbows bore down, giving each of us the added leverage we pursued. We needed to be closer to Mom and to the steaming platter she placed before us. Under the creamy glow of the kitchen light, six accepting eyes took in the uncomplicated joy and radiance emanating from Mom as she sought the simple, albeit little-known and usually wasted, prize this creature offered. Our eager young faces beamed, hearts alight with happiness, senses fully alert, mimicking Mom's contagious aura. This was a moment frozen in time—the anticipation of what was soon to be savored. Without question, we would like this stuff, if by no other means than through osmosis. That's the way it was; we were caught up and swept along in a euphoric stream of family emotion.

As I recall, it was a sort of serrated, grapefruit-type carving spoon that Mom used to ease both delicate morsels, now baked to perfection, off the concave structure they occupied. As my mother served each piece, she looked radiant, hazel eyes dancing under brunette bangs softly sweeping her brow on the left. She knew this taste, fragrant with a hint of rosemary and lemon, was exquisite.

Her lips rounding, a moist and velvety flow of air breaking into an impassioned murmur, "Oooh, uummm," as the air resonating from her throat rolled over her tongue, buoyed by the juice of a thousand taste buds tingling in anticipation. This image is indelibly etched in my mind as Mom prepared to partake and share with us this simple pleasure of life. I can only believe this was the sound of an enraptured soul. If a soul can be heard, I imagine it would speak to me in just such a way as my mother's unconscious response on those occasions.

Mom didn't stand on formality on an everyday basis. That's why elbows on the table and pork chop bones sucked clean could easily figure into casual mealtime in our house. So in her easy way, after she had retrieved the first morsel, she'd hold it gently between her fingers and sit there a moment, completely mesmerized, basking in the beauty of the moment. Then she'd say in a gleeful whisper as she carefully split the sumptuous bit apart, "You're just not going to believe it, my darlings. How good this is. It's a delicacy. The tenderloin!"

And to our delight she tenderly placed a piece between the waiting lips of two of us, then quickly secured the second and last piece between her fingers to divide for the third one of us kids and herself. Softly chuckling, she'd slowly, reverently eat her melt-in-your-mouth morsel. We three would giggle in agreement, licking our lips.

I luxuriate in the memory of how Mom taught us the art of honoring and eating fish cheeks. She held in high esteem those scrumptious delicacies making up the cheeks of fish, just as I hold dear this particular memory of her. I've come to appreciate the fact that the fish needs some size or, believe me, you won't find much cheek. I know that the largeness of those special moments with Mom added enormous spiritual weight to each cheek.

It didn't dawn on me before her spirit left her body to find out who had taught her to eat fish cheeks, so that bit of knowledge is lost and will forever remain a mystery to me. But the ritual has been passed on to my children.

It's funny how folks pick up ideas, use them for awhile, and then innocently claim them as their own. Years later, after my husband had long been enmeshed in our fish cheek feasting, I heard him mention to our youngest that the gift of eating fish cheeks had been passed down from his mother. I was speechless, but in honor of my mother, I had to set the record straight. Words found their way, and in the end he sheepishly conceded that it was my mother who was our fish cheek guru.

Photo contributed by Lynn: Mom and Dad before he left.
The world's mine oyster. ~William Shakespeare

Lynn Henriksen: "As a daughter, niece, sister, friend, wife, mother, and grandmother, and through many wonderful years guiding people of all ages to write memoir, I find the greatest truth and beauty lie in the extraordinary ordinary."

Back to truth and imagination, there may be times when you are relating incidents that someone else told you about your grandmother, for instance—that would be hearsay—but it's all right to use that information, too, if you feel comfortable with it and it is integral to your story. It is only when you change events that you are veering from the truth. And it's okay to change names to protect the *innocent*, in fact, it may be necessary. Take a little poetic license, use your imagination. Remember, you are looking for truths that you remember—memoir is neither a newspaper article, nor is it the official version of a story, it is the true version seen through your eyes.

Mine memory gems. Touch the textured surfaces of your mind first to loosen and then to absorb the sensory details. Enrich your story by imagining and describing...

- the scents lingering in the air in your grandmother's kitchen.
- the look on your mother's face when she held fast to her principles.
- the hissing sounds of the factory presses where mom toiled each day to make ends meet.
- the taste of mom's secret recipe rhubarb pie.
- the cool, smoothness of the aging skin on the back of grandma's hands.

It's now time for intuition to make a grand entrance. Where does intuition come in? Most everywhere. Many of us have simply not learned to recognize it for what it is. Some call it our sixth sense, others say ESP (extrasensory perception), and I've heard it referred to as spiritual recognition. I'll stick with intuition here; although, the various references apply depending upon one's belief system or understand of the sixth sense.

The following definition comes from intuitionworks.com: The word intuition comes from the Latin intueri, meaning to consider, to look on. This intuitive "look on" implies something deeper than simple perception and is best described as apperception, the ability to "take hold of" knowledge in one glance. Webster's Dictionary sums up intuition as "the immediate knowing or learning of something without the conscious use of reasoning; instantaneous apperception." Simply stated, intuition is direct knowledge. Intuition reflects your ability to go inward, respond to a variety of intuitive skills, perceive connections, communicate nontraditionally, and tap personal and collective wisdom.

Whether you realize it or not, intuition is a part of what you will use when you tell your truths by tapping into personal memories to make connections, all the while subconsciously relying on personal and collective wisdom. Intuition coupled with imagination is even more subtle and intangible than are the five physical senses that we use to bridge memory to story.

Since we can't perceive the physical effects of these intangibles in any way other than looking inward to intuit events, we might think they're not a reliable indication of the actions we want to put forth as truth in our stories. I don't see it that way. In fact, I think it is impossible not to use the vast possibilities of our sixth sense when we tap memory and write memoir. Intuitive insights should be used as building blocks for further reasoning, so go ahead—enjoy fully using all six of your senses as you write. You can write a scene with the help of a composite picture put together from various ideas and avenues of information gathering. What you've learned by personal experience, family stories, and from your favorite books will give you ample sources upon which to draw.

Virginia Woolf said that every time a woman writes she goes back through all her mothers. Do this—go back through all the "knowing" that is deep inside your bones to combine both the intuitive and the experiential. Ask for help from the ancestral line of your soul, the place where answers can be found.

SIXTH SENSE

There are myriad ways to define the sixth sense, but I think calling it intuition is the simplest interpretation. Intuition is a link to an awareness outside the physical realm; it is direct insight, without employing rational analysis. Moreover, it adds another dimension to perception when it is integrated with the physical senses of sight, taste, touch, smell, and hearing. Intuition, the sixth sense, is not to be confused with basic instinct, rather it is a "knowing" with a spiritual element.

You rely on your sixth sense without realizing it most of the time. When you are sensitive to things around you, which you can't discover through physical stimuli, you are using your sixth sense to inform you of what is going on. For example, your intuition tells you someone is following you, even though you can't see, hear, touch, smell, or taste that someone—you simply know she is there—you sense it.

> **FREE WRITE:** By continuing to stay open to
> insight and answers that come to you freely
> through all six of your senses, write down several
> instances from your past where you recognize that
> intuition mingled with your physical senses to
> heighten awareness. Now use what you have
> discovered to rewrite passages in your memoir by
> combining the intuitive with the physical.

TellTale Soul Bunny Conlon's remembrance, below, illustrates
a rhythm of passion flowing from deep inside her mother's spirit
as she took a knowing stand.

Taking a Stand

~Bunny Conlon

*Probably my earliest memory, or at least the most important from a
moral point of view, is of an event that occurred in a grocery store. I was
perhaps four years old at the time and my pregnant mother, with her three
children in tow, had just been taxed to the max while grocery shopping.*

*My older sister, who had me convinced that she was the head of the
family, had talked Mother, a woman well-known for her acquiescence, into
filling our basket with things we could have lived without. My brother,
pushing the basket and making motor noises as five-year-old boys will do,
had nearly brought Mom to tears by running into her Achilles' heel too
many times as she studied the grocery shelves for the ingredients she needed to
prepare our meals for the coming week. I, being the perfect child (although a
little "spaced out"), had managed to get lost among the aisles in the store
and found myself holding the hand of a kindly but unknown person. I
reacted normally by screaming bloody murder, which promptly brought my
poor, frantic mother to my rescue (or perhaps to the rescue of the frightened*

and embarrassed woman whose only intention was to help me locate my family).

Now we were standing in the checkout line in Grand Prairie, Texas, the year was 1945. There was a couple in front of us. They had a baby and a toddler. They were black and something was wrong. My mom shushed us so she could hear what the store clerk was saying to them. Tears welled up in the black lady's eyes. Her husband was very angry. The tension was thick and the children began to cry and cling tightly to their mother. They left their basket of food at the head of the line and departed. My mother was next up.

I recall so clearly looking up at Mom. She had never looked so tall, so strong, and so beautiful as she did at that moment. She said to the clerk in a louder voice than I ever remember hearing her use before or after, "If you can't accept their money, you cannot have mine, either."

My mother collected the three of us children, and we proudly followed her out of the store. I knew then that I had picked the right mother.

Photo contributed by Bunny: Mom age 17.

Bunny Conlon: "I've spent most of my days in the Land of Enchantment. I married, gave birth to a precious son, was widowed, and remarried, finding true love twice in one lifetime."

ADDING SPARKS, SPONTANEITY, AND STYLE

You are writing creative nonfiction to tell an appealing true story in an engaging manner, not writing an operational manual for Smartphone users or reporting the results of an election on a political blog. You will create a *Mother Memoir* that resembles fiction in the way it is written by embellishing scenes with stimulating details, describing the captivating dash of your character's personality, and by making the incident or event intriguing through the use of sparks that ignite passion. Often times the best way to learn is by example.

As you read the three stories that follow, note the unique styles of Marie, Ruth, and Marlene, as each *TellTale Soul* uses rich dashes to ignite passion as understanding unfolds. Doing so will help you create depth, design, and color as you rework the draft of your emerging story.

Rich dashes...

Harvesting Tranquility
~Marie de la Paz Baires

The earthenware crock stretched further across than my arms could reach and was just deep enough. It sat next to the oven she had made by digging out earth to make a hole that would contain the perfect wood fire. For how long she had been preparing the ingredients and cooking at the fires I do not like to think, but it was for Christmas week feasting. Always tamales— chicken tamales. Hundreds of tamales with the magnificent, delicious aroma of steeping banana leaf mingling with that of chicken and cornmeal. All the family would be coming—the grandparents, aunties and uncles, and all the children. It was a happy time; there would be much hugging at the midnight of Christmas. But there were many years of great effort before my mother had the luxury of filling a crock such as that.

My mother, thank God, is still living, and her life is not so hard now. When my husband and I came to the United States seven years ago to find more opportunity, our two daughters stayed behind in Mami's care. They live together still in the same small fishing village on the Pacific Ocean in El Salvador that we left so long ago (I have not been able to go back.). I remember Mami standing tall and proud on strong legs and sturdy feet with her long, shiny dark hair wound in a bun. We are very similar, only my hair is worn back in a braid straight down my back, and she is more subdued than I, but also a happy person – our different personalities came out, that is all.

We were her six children; she sat us down and told us how her life had been. A very sad past, but she was not ashamed, because through all hardships she learned to value life and appreciate what came to her. My mother told me that they were seven children, so she had to work from a very early age to help my abuela with the younger children. Mami went to school only for one year. She grew up very poor, without even a place to live. She agonized over having no home. But there was nothing to do except face the situation. After she married my father, they had few resources to offer their own children. That was the greatest of concerns to my beautiful Mother.

She is a very knowing woman, and for that reason my father loves her very much. Mami forced herself to work very hard in her struggle to provide for even our most basic of needs. With God's help, and my mother's diligence, we came to have a different life, one she always wanted for her family. She was determined that her children would learn to read and write.

She worked like a man at my father's side in the fields of beans and rice and corn, planting seeds, tending the crops, and finally harvesting what had grown. At four o'clock each morning, well before the sun rose, while all the family slept, she alone began the gentle rolling out of the tortillas that would sustain her family for the day. Eventually we acquired a home in which there was no abundance of material things, but there was love and great peace and tranquility.

My mother is a poor but courageous woman who lives with great honor and holds much virtue within. She is far from common—a thoughtful woman. And she knows the ways.

Marie de la Paz Baires: "Mami, you are too far away, but I keep you close in my heart."

Passion ignites…

The Funeral Cake

~Ruth Francke

I always cry at funerals. Sometimes I don't even know the deceased, but the way I come apart you'd think I'd lost my own true love. But then I did lose my greatest love much too early. At each funeral I see myself as the eight-year-old standing at Mother's grave. Is it self-pity or regret?

I remember a lot from my eight years with her. She was born in East Prussia and lived through two wars. I know there was great hardship, but she managed to walk on the sunny side of life most of the time. My mother was wonderful.

Our lessons as children grew from the necessity of invention and imagination, Mother's "seven-tails," the sorting and sifting of moral dilemmas, and the Brothers Grimm and Hauff. There was not much to pilfer on the Eastern Front, but Mother saw to it that I had one rather disproportioned doll, which she'd concocted from several others of different sizes and styles. But my brother and I derived the most fun from the games we invented as our imaginations soared with the stimulation from our greatest joy—Mother's reading of the nightly before-bed stories.

155

We'd heard all the Brothers had to tell a thousand times, but each night we'd comfortably establish ourselves around the huge tile oven to listen to our mother read once more the tales, none without a moral. I'd sit on the back of Mother's armchair, my legs dangling over her shoulders, and braid her hair while she read.

The same stories over and over must have bored her to tears, but she read them to us with verve. Their messages were often brutal, but they were effective. Child psychologists today cringe at them, but I believe the fairy tales contributed positively to our moral and ethical development. I remember "Struwelpeter" who refused to wash and comb his hair or cut his nails. One day he met the barber, who, in attempting to trim Peter's hair with gigantic scissors, cut off Peter's head because his face no longer could be seen through the dirt and tangled hair.

Some might question my mother's moral teachings, but she did what she had to do to keep us healthy during terrible times. Mother took us on long walks, usually with a purpose: We would look in on this farm or that, while Mother charmed eggs and lard and bacon from the farm women who seemed to revel in the gracious, animated words that so easily rolled off her well-educated tongue.

We were forced to stretch honesty in those days of meager rations— practically everything went to the front. But my mother taught my brother and me the difference between stealing and taking. The former would land us in jail for sure, but with the latter we had more leeway should we be caught. Occasionally freight cars stopped on the tracks outside our town on their way to Stargard. Should some of the contents spill through the door, it was okay to collect them; but to open the door wider and help ourselves would be considered a crime. If we were lucky, we might carry home more sugar beets than our little bodies could endure; Mother knew how to extract sweet, black molasses from them and fashion a kind of candy for us.

Punishment wasn't handed out often in our home—even though I think we were impish little brats—but when it was, discipline came to us through the seven-tails: Seven thin leather strips, knotted at the ends, were attached to a handle, which Mother held as she whacked us over our behinds— always both of us, either because we both deserved it or because one came whining about the other's misdeeds. Naturally we screamed bloody murder before she could inflict any real pain.

She had nerves of steel, so we got away with a lot. I liked to snip the edges of tablecloths to make fringes, braid the fringes together and then snip the braids off. I can't ever remember being slapped in the face, but I had my fingers slapped for snipping the tablecloths.

Once I lay in bed with scarlet fever for what seemed an endless time, and to keep me there was no easy feat. Mother surprised me with a huge pancake the "mailman" had delivered. In it I found small gift-wrapped packages with treats, heaven knows whom she charmed to obtain those little gifts. I was occupied for a while. My mother was filled with love (although she despised Hitler) and had ever-present optimism which is one of the legacies that I am most thankful for.

She also was compassionate, once harboring a gravely ill runaway soldier in our house for days. She asked no questions, accommodating him on the sofa until he died of cholera. The stench of his feces permeated the air in our place for weeks afterwards, even though mother sprinkled the last drops of her treasured bottle of perfume where she could. Mother had been in pain and had been suffering off and on for months herself, so she empathized with his plight.

Sometimes my brother and I would find Mother on the sofa, in a tight little ball, clenching her stomach. We'd do our best to go about finding something for supper. One time I came in and my mother said with the slightest reproach in her voice, "I heard you shouting and laughing and you did not hear me call. I am so thirsty." That was the only time she ever asked something of me and I was not there for her. I am still crying.

She died in hospital of kidney failure and leukemia eight days after her birthday on June 16, 1945. When I saw Mother last, two days before she died, she said that she had baked a cake for us and pointed toward the big tile heatstove in the corner of the hospital room. As long as I live, I will never forget that beautiful cake.

Lynn Cook Henriksen

Photo courtesy of Ruth: My mother.

Ruth Francke: "Uprooted by the war, the soul of our family
gone, we lived a gypsy life like roommates, each with his
responsibilities. Having lived in various places in Germany and
France, trying also the States comes hardly as a surprise. Even
here I resided in the South, the East, and settled in San
Francisco—for now... Home is where I hang my hat."

Understanding unfolds...

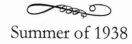

Summer of 1938

~Marlene Mason

My mother nearly died when she was thirteen. She wasn't hit by a car. She wasn't thrown from a horse. She didn't contract pneumonia. Death would come for my mother, violently, painfully, slowly moving up her body, wracking it, torturously traveling through her nervous system, breaking bones, nearly starving her, and refusing to give its name.

Now, seventy-one years later, if I'm careful and quiet, she will visit that past. I'm glad she doesn't move there, for I can only imagine what it was like to live through it once.

The summer of 1938 was just like many other summers in my mother's young life, filled with sunshine, swimming, lounging along the shore on Liberty Lake, Washington, nights spent dancing at the Dance Pavilion (my mother so loves to dance) and helping her grandparents run the bathhouse and boat docks at Dreamwood Bay. As she talks about this part of her story, it sounds an idyllic life. I can see her now, slender, freckle-faced, flaming red hair, clear blue eyes sparkling with laughter. Her nickname, Polly, short for Pollyanna, fits her even now, these many years later.

Running home, barefoot, with her sister from the lake one day, she races across the yard. Her small dog, Boots, was often found there chewing on a bone. A bone splinter pierced deeply into her foot. And Death has slipped in unseen. The splinter was removed, the foot soaked in Lysol water, bandaged and forgotten. School was beginning soon and life went on.

Polly was entering eighth grade. Rather a shy, and very modest, young girl, she remembers how two boys in her multi-grade class began to taunt her, calling her stupid and laughing at her as she struggled with her lessons. As I've come to know more about her ordeal, I can only wonder if it was the fatigue and headaches already portending the tragedy ahead, that so challenged her ability to learn. She tells me she was tormented by their mockery. I can still hear the wound in her tone.

Her humiliation in class was merely a prelude of what was to come. After only two weeks of school she would have to drop out due to extreme fatigue. Shortly thereafter things became markedly worse. She was bed-ridden; barely able to open her mouth the width of her baby finger and no longer able to eat; no one could determine what was wrong.

The agonizing muscle spasms began, the worst of which was while my mother sat on the toilet with the aid of my grandmother. So frail was she by now, she couldn't make it to the bathroom on her own. I know my mother well enough to know this was an immense embarrassment to her. As her muscles wrenched her small body rigid as an ironing board, my mother's spine was slammed against the wooden flush box, crushing two vertebras in her upper back. I feel the horror in my heart though I sense only flatness in hers.

I am stunned. I had not known this part of the story. "My god, Mom, that must have been excruciating," I say. She says "No, I don't remember that it was." This statement tells me in full measure of the agony already being endured. I still don't know, and I cannot ask, for fear the answer will sicken me further, if this injury was ever treated. Obviously, the poison in her body was far more life-threatening; everything else a moot point.

The Great Depression had not ended for my mother's family. Doctors were a luxury, though there was no longer any doubt a doctor's expertise was required. My mother was not getting better. She was getting much, much worse. Her small body shrinking in its racking agony, and no one knew what could possibly be the matter.

My mom still has vivid memories of a female physician coming to the house to examine her and attempting to pry her mouth open with a spoon. I feel sick to my stomach as I listen. I can hear the nausea in her own voice as she tells me she's just grateful her teeth, or worse, her jaw, were not broken. This physician went away, leaving my mother still undiagnosed.

My mother believes in miracles; she has experienced a few. A neighbor happened to be a former military doctor. He'd seen cases of tetanus, or lockjaw, as it is sometimes called, in the military and ordered my mom be taken immediately to the hospital in Spokane. Now Death has a name and it is dreadfully near.

The memories are fresh when she speaks of feeling like a human pin cushion from the many, many needles driven into her. She remembers well the bruises. She remembers, too, feeling her feet begin to go numb; the numbness inching up her legs, as paralysis slowly crept through her muscles. She remembers losing control of her bowels and bladder as poison advanced throughout her body. She remembers her mortification when she lost control of her bladder and wet the bed as her eldest brother stood at her bedside. I ache at her suffering. She aches with her shame.

Sacred Heart Catholic Hospital, in Spokane, had no tetanus immune globulin on hand for some unknown reason and none was, apparently, to be found anywhere nearby. I am grateful it was developed in 1891, though it appeared it wasn't going to do my mother much good. All hope was forsaken, and, though not Catholic, she was given Last Rites by a priest.

As luck, or another miracle, would have it, New York City had the life-saving serum if only it could be gotten to my mother, some three thousand miles away. My Uncle Sterling, in the Navy at the time, was stationed on the East Coast. Taking emergency leave, he flew to New York, collected the serum, racing against time to, literally, snatch his baby sister from Death's close grasp. I do not wonder he was her hero ever after. Today he is mine as well.

The story does not end happily here. I've since read the heartbreaking muscle spasms related to lockjaw will decrease in about two weeks and disappear entirely after three or four. I cannot imagine how she was able to endure such prolonged suffering. Moments of intense pain are endless; weeks unfathomable to me. Thankfully, little of that seems to be a part of my mother's memory. According to her, "she simply remained in the hospital for two weeks." Research tells me she probably suffered far more than she recalls.

While she slowly regained her health and some of the weight she'd lost, her spine would never be straight again, creating a small hunch between her brave shoulders. I had previously believed it was caused by osteoporosis.

Her amazing recovery still wasn't the end of her degrading experiences. The lockjaw had, for reasons the medical profession did not understand, caused her ribs to collapse inward. I now believe it was the untreated, undiagnosed, crushed vertebrae causing the deformity, but I don't know if that was ever determined. Her doctors asked her to be a case study in order to scrutinize her condition in hopes of better understanding this horrendous disease. She was brought before a medical convention, hundreds of doctors in attendance, set upon a stage, partially covered with a sheet insufficient to protect her modesty…and studied. At thirteen years old she was mortified, but she permitted it, she says, "to help others." It was here, in front of these many men, she would experience her first menstrual period. She still blushes, hangs her head and lowers her voice at the remembrance.

Her memory holds many moments of 1938, the year she began wearing glasses, her favorite sister gave birth to a daughter, and my mother rubbed shoulders with death; today she speaks of it all with a certain wonder in her voice. She recalls the relief she experienced when returning to school some five months after the onset of tetanus, to find the tormenting boys had moved on to high school. Though they were gone, she was never able to dispel their cruel taunts. I cannot help but wonder how her horrific illness was affecting her mind and body at that time, in that classroom. Those boys were quite likely seeing the effect of the venomous bacterium coursing through her. The injury they inflicted was perhaps as painful as the disease, and I would like to believe they would be mournfully sorry today if they only knew the hurt they'd caused.

My mother amazes me over and over again with each new skill she acquires, each added responsibility she assumes since my father's death, with the strength of character she consistently demonstrates. Though her curved spine still tells the tale of her ordeal, her "backbone" is straight and strong! She seems taller to me now than ever before. There have been times when I have forgotten I am not the elder adult and thought I knew what she should do. She has left me little doubt she could, and would, knock some sense into me should it be needed. She is fierce, a fighter and I know what strength is there.

My mom and I have traveled over sixty years together. Though it has not been a smooth path, nor always parallel, we have arrived at "Best Friends," a gift I cherish beyond words. I am honored when she tells me she feels the same.

Photo Contributed by Marlene: Marlene (Stead).

Marlene Mason: "In writing this story about my mother, I was surprised and in awe of her courage and stoic demeanor. I had never thought of my mother as a strong, courageous, determined person. This story peeled away the limited blinders through which I'd previously seen my mother and brought us even closer to each other's hearts."

Take some time here to reflect on what these three *TellTale Souls* so amply revealed to you in the stories above. Go over these questions in your mind as you consider each story:

> ➢ How do I feel about each *Mother Memoir* specifically?
> ➢ What pictures come to mind about their mothers?
> ➢ Which words, phrases, and images convey the storytellers' messages?
> ➢ What makes me smile, frown, or empathize?

> ➤ What makes me remember?
> ➤ What makes these women come alive for me?
> ➤ What sense do I have of these women, and why?
> ➤ Do I find a common bond?
> ➤ Could any of the voices have been mine?
> ➤ Do these mother figures remind me of anyone?

WRITE: Weave more details into your story, adding rich dashes and passion that ignites. Afterward, take the time to realize what this adventure in writing has led you to understand.

Allow spontaneity to guide your work. Just because you like the way someone else describes a situation, that form may or may not be your style. Don't let your writing become contrived. Don't force it; it will come into its own as you continue to write. Be true to whom you are and to the style that naturally flows from you; let it come out from within. Looking inward to the intuitive you allows you to express yourself with honesty and respect.

It is advantageous, however, not only to read your favorite authors often, but also to seek out new authors whose voices resonate with your voice so that you become more and more comfortable with the styles that inspire you. You might say, "I don't know what my style is." It bears repeating that your individual or natural style will become apparent the more you write because it is an evolution. By trusting in the spontaneity of the process, your style will make itself known. Something else to realize is that your style will mirror the way you discuss issues, talk with your neighbors or your loved ones, and write letters or make notes in a diary. Even the way you drive your car or make love demonstrates how you naturally communicate.

TellTale Soul Mary's *Mother Memoir* is a poignant, intimate letter to her mum.

Dear Mum

~Mary Wilkinson

How fitting it is that I am writing this letter to you stretched out on the floor as I so often did when I was a child. Do you remember how you used to laugh and remark that I could never sit on a chair for long? Somehow, it feels like the right thing to do today, to be lying beside the fire, with the crackle of wood in the grate and the constant tap-dance of raindrops against glass.

Mum, so much time has passed since we've last spoken. I miss you, but you know that, don't you. There are times when I still cannot believe you are gone. I like to think that you are on a long journey and you will come back, not soon, but sometime. There is no other possibility in my concept of your absence, no finality to you not being here.

I am sure I never thanked you properly for all those things that are far too numerous to list. Some do keep replaying in my mind though, like an old movie reel that sputters and flickers in a darkened room. Your hands appear on the screen immediately, you're seldom idle, always fixing, making, baking, stroking, elegant hands that tended without a hint of hesitation. And your footfall on the stairs that caused the fourth step up to creak as you bring a blue mug of steaming cocoa to my sick bed. I see you in the kitchen too, with the wide expanse of cotton sheets between us as we unravel and stretch, match and fold.

There is a day where the frame momentarily stalls, and Mum, you lean against a whitewashed wall, bordered by red fuchsia, a rare stillness to your being, as if you are gleaning strength from the sunshine that falls on your face, your eyes closed in meditation, like a basking cat purring on a windowsill. And there we are, in the balm of a summer's night, strolling beside the sea, a shared bag of French fries, the tang of vinegar on our lips, bare feet dusted with sand.

There are occasions when darkness crops up in this old movie reel. I recall Mum, how you cried with frustration at the hard times. I never knew exactly what those hard times were, but I can guess now, guess that holding it all in was not such a good idea after all. You had your fair share of disappointment and regret too, didn't you? I know how you had longed to emigrate to Canada when you first married Dad. I know how you wished that you had learnt to drive. I know too, that Dad wasn't always that easy to live with and, yet, you struggled on with what circumstances life doled out. Dear stoic Mum. I recall you telling me once that when you first married, how there was little money to spend. That you had to survive without a washing machine and a dryer for years and there was no alternative but to handwash the clothes, dry them by the fire. Years later, you often laughed and remarked about the irony of it all, that when you finally had money to spend, there was nothing you desired.

You told me too, that I should never entertain malice or bitterness. You said that it would only show on the face. So is that why you had the most beautiful skin? Flawless, soft and sweet smelling of roses. Even in the hospital room, on one of those last precious visits, before you went away. Even though your body had changed, so tiny and fragile it was, sparrow-like for all the world, that for a moment, I actually wondered if it was really you at all. Until I got up close that is, and felt the brush of your skin against mine. It was still soft and strangely reminiscent. Reminiscent of your life, the indelible stamp etched on your face. It was in the way you strove to look on the bright side of circumstance, as much as you could and how you gave away without expecting anything in return. It was also in the way you called me to you that day, how you patted the sheet and whispered, "Come over to me love," and as I did, you turned your palm, upward and out. You were trusting me to come and you were trusting the long road you had travelled and the journey that beckoned.

Photo Courtesy of Mary: Mum patching my knee, County Galway, Ireland.

Mary Wilkinson: "I would be delighted if that photo of Mum fixing my knee at the old kitchen table was included.... My god, she would have been honoured."

Each of you sees the world and all of its wonders and creatures, great and small, in your own way. Each of you will write a distinctive story, even the same story would be told by each of you in a very different way—each to his own, you might say. How interesting it is to recognize that no one else can do just exactly what you do no matter how hard they might try. Celebrate your individuality.

Funny, isn't it, you probably don't tell the same exact story twice yourself. There is a great line in the movie, *The Lives of Others*, where an interrogator explains that you can tell when a prisoner is lying if he tells his story or answers questions exactly the same way each time he is asked. It seems if we have not memorized an incident that we're relating to another person, it will come out slightly changed each time we talk about it.

The more you have listened to the people and the world around you and the more perceptive your eye and ear, the better your communication style will be. In addition, the more you listen with your ear turned inward, open to the vast untapped universe within, the more authentic a writer you will become. A memorable, arousing tale will unfold when you let it. And the power of your story will come when you give it your all, your way—tell it until it hurts or sets you free.

Have you ever wondered if other women's stories are there to

seek us out, to lead us to the discovery that

we are at once one and all?

Lynn Cook Henriksen

For a long time now I have tried simply to write the best I can. Sometimes I have good luck and write better than I can.

~ Ernest Hemingway

Act Four

Society has framed us in, directed we plot out our lives through three acts or stages: youth, middle age, and old age. We'd be mad as Hatters if we settled for that form of confinement. Out with that notion—there's more to us than that.

Looking toward freedom of expression, Act Four centers around an energizing time in the life of your writing where you will take a close look at how your Mother Memoir is shaping up, and how you will cleverly respond to ideas to buzz it up. Little Alice, back in Wonderland, had the opportunity to enter into parts of herself she wasn't yet aware and view alternatives to walking the well worn path of her time. You have had the same chance Alice had, as you journeyed through Acts One, Two, and Three, to look at your mother and yourself in ways you never before imagined. Now, go create an even better story...

FINISHING TOUCHES

Don't stop now. It's time to add the finishing touches to your bio-vignette by taking an even closer look at certain aspects of your writing and at the leading character, your mother, who holds a hugely significant place in your life. Remember when you infused imagination into the body of your story in Act Three? Well, it is time for your imagination to attract even more attention to the strokes in your story.

You have made excellent progress up to this point focusing on finding your voice, writing creatively, looking at truth and imagination, using elements of intuition, and developing your main character's spirit by getting to the core of whom she is or was. I wanted you to feel secure connecting on the deepest of levels with your memories, finding the bones of your story, and writing from your heart, prior to giving your story a once over using even more exploratory writing techniques.

People seek entertainment, knowledge, and/or connection when they read creative nonfiction, and it is essential for them to feel emotionally engaged or they won't care what you have to say. I believe it's now time to work on the finishing touches that will span your entire story from beginning to end. What I mean by finishing touches runs from how you start your story, use sensory hooks to enliven characters, weave complexity through emotion, to setting your memoir in time and place. Be sure to pay special attention to the essence of your mother, the very heart of your story, as you craft each area you revisit. Here are eighteen little words that fully engage my emotions:

She had a curious way of lifting roses by the chin
to look them full in the face.
~Colette, recalling her mother, Sido

Sidonie Gabrielle Colette went on to say, after reflecting on writing about her mother, "I am not at all sure that I have put the finishing touches to these portraits of her; nor am I at all sure that I have discovered all that she has bequeathed to me. I have come late to this task. But where could I find a better one for my last?"

Those sentiments ring true for all *TellTale Souls*; it is comforting to know we are in the company of one of the world's great writers when we are writing about our mothers. Although it is not particularly easy for any of us to give up our stories—the tales seem never quite polished enough to do *her* justice—please know that you can accomplish what you set out to do by simply doing your best to add the finished touches to your *Mother Memoir*. What more could any mother ask?

I have asked you to put yourself in your mother's shoes. This time I suggest you put yourself in the shoes of the daughter in the following heartfelt bio-vignette. In approximately 1,200 words, which I wrote for Joyce after a lengthy interview, she told me I captured her sentiments completely.

And the Music Stopped

~Joyce Turley

The music, her playing classical music on our baby grand lulled me to sleep every night of my life until I was thirteen and a half-years-old. And, in the middle of the night when the fairies dance, I dreamed of flying off with my mother to a happy place filled with nothing but sunshine and fun.

She had the prettiest teeth I have ever seen. This five foot tall, free-spirited mother of mine was a brunette, a light-skinned, blue-eyed beauty, who didn't really look Italian. She got more than her share of attention from men; she made their heads turn when she walked into a room or down the street. I've often wondered if it was because she was so beautiful that she had such a love of beautiful things and wanted to make more of her place in life than it actually was.

Long before the music stopped, she instilled in me a love of music and art. By the time I was five years old, I remember wanting to be an actress, not a pianist, even though my mother had me playing a simplified version of Beethoven's Minuet in G by that time. Mother was a concert pianist on a small scale; beyond giving me a classical piano lesson every day, she earned thirty-five cents an hour giving lessons in our house during the great depression, which she would take to the Savings & Loan to deposit in her "escape" account.

As I grew older, I remember playing duo piano, my treble to Mother's bass; we'd pound on the keys, and I'd sing all the popular songs, and we had such fun. She was a happy lady, but complained about her marriage to my father. And, I have to say, I discovered she fibbed some to make her fantasy world more a reality. She visualized a more intellectual life than she led. She wanted this life so badly that she made up a world in which she lived that wasn't exactly real. I think she always knew she'd make a major escape to be with people who had more of what she was interested in and where she could realize her dreams.

My father was proud of my mother for her refinement and attractiveness and musical talent, but he didn't know how to handle it or her, so he came off as domineering. In fact, I believe he thought he'd won the brass ring when my mother agreed to marry him. Sadly, it didn't take long for my mother to feel unhappily married, but she became pregnant with my older brother, so she stayed with my dad. He bought her an upright piano, which fit snuggly against the living room wall, so she could lose herself in her music; that sufficed until the baby grand piano, my grandmother actually bought for me on my seventh birthday, arrived and took up most of the room. My mother took up all her spare time at the keyboard until the day the music stopped.

Pearl Harbor was stealthily bombed by the Japanese early one Sunday morning on the island of Oahu, shocking and shaking our Nation momentarily to its collective knees in December of 1941, ushering in the cacophony of World War II; a war that would last for four agonizing years. Just one month later, in the dusk of early night one January evening of 1942, in Easton, Pennsylvania, my mother donned her black wool coat and tied a soft silk scarf carefully around her hair before slipping soundlessly out of the house to go to "meet" Clark Gable at the movies. She'd mentioned earlier in the day that she planned to see a movie that evening after dinner. There were no good-byes to my father, brother, or to me. I went to bed in the quiet, no music by which to dream, unaware that my mother's music had stopped for all time in our old Pennsylvania house; she never came back when I was thirteen and a half-years-old.

She'd threatened to leave many times throughout the years, saying she'd take me with her, but my brother was to stay with our father. To say her abandonment brought me to my knees would not be true, since I told myself, I believed, she was a butterfly who needed to fly away. I knew she loved me. Somehow I understood something unspoken about her, but to this day I've always had to have a baby grand in my home whether or not I had the room or money for it, and even though I seldom play.

I don't know why she didn't take me with her, and I didn't ask her when she called several weeks after she left to ask me to pack her clothes and send them to her. I cleaned out my piggy bank to get the money, and because my instincts told me my father shouldn't know what was going on, I walked the twenty blocks, broken piggy in hand, to the post office to mail one brown cardboard box to an address in Danville, New Jersey, I'd scribbled down. That was it, until nearly four years later, when the Seventeen Magazine subscription was sent to me on my seventeenth birthday, I suspect that it came from her, even though the sender line was left blank.

~~~

Twenty-five years later I moved back to Pennsylvania from California, which was many years after I'd read the obituary a relative had sent me marking my mother's passing in Danville, New Jersey. The obituary mentioned the generous donation my mother had made to her Catholic church by having bells built for it replicating the bells she'd fallen in love

175

with while teaching in Italy, on what I can only assume must have been one of her butterfly migrations.

One day soon after moving back East, my husband, Fred, and I were driving down the freeway when I noticed the Danville exit sign at exactly the same time my husband maneuvered to take the exit ramp. Obviously our thinking was in sync, we were headed for the church where she'd had the bells installed. Miraculously, as we drove up the lane, we heard music; the bells were ringing in all their glory. The saying rings true, this was music to my ears; music from my mother once again.

Fast forward another thirty years, I'm talking with our priest friend in Eureka, California, and he says, "My bells in the church have stopped ringing; the parishioners are sad that the music stopped." Fred and I looked at each other, once again in sync, knowing this was our cue; we would replicate these bells for our friend's Catholic church. The music of the bells will soon ring coast to coast to honor both of our mothers.

Just this past year, while our priest was still investigating the best method to duplicate or rebuild the bells, my dear Fred died. I recently finished what we started, and I can imagine his smile spreading from ear to ear as the bells toll strong and clear for him, too.

Photo contributed by Joyce: My brother, Mother, and I.

176

Joyce Turley: "My life is rich, full of travel and businesses and children and friends. I'm a professional speaker and an author—the current book is *Brownie Points.* And of this much I am sure, whether we have our mothers for thirteen years or sixty years, aren't we always sitting at the window waiting for her to walk around the bend?"

Imagine your mother reading your telling tale. What would she think about the way you described her physical characteristics and emotional reactions? Imagining Mom reading about herself through your eyes can stimulate you to be a better writer by prompting you to place just the right spark here and there. You already know how to spice up your life and surroundings in various ways: I would be willing to bet, when many of you decorate your homes, you spend a good deal of time figuring out which decorative pillow will create the perfect atmospheric touch; when planting your gardens, you mix contrasting shades of colorful leaves and flowers to produce that Wow! effect; or when dressing up to go out for the evening, you try on more than one outfit and make sure your lipstick doesn't clash with your new orange sweater before you set one well-clad foot out the door. Whichever way you visualize your mother, as a fragrant jasmine, thorny rose, or someone in between, it is up to you to do her and your story justice by enhancing it in style.

Before we begin investigating story starters in the next section, **WRITE** a couple paragraphs musing over what you think your mother would say about how you have described her so far in your story.

RUNNING WITH STORY STARTERS

Make the most of your power of imagination by thinking of creative ways to catch readers—set the bait, hook them, reel them in.

JOT DOWN your answers to two simple questions:
1) What does the first paragraph in a story have to do or say to entice me to continue reading?
2) How can I best use my imagination to put the necessary enticement, the bait, in the first several lines of my tale?

Openings must command attention by attracting interest, and they must lure the reader in an anticipatory manner for your story to be successful. Think of your story starter as the *hook* songwriters use to grab your ear, to make you want to listen to more of the lyrics. You need a few intriguing opening sentences for someone to want to go on reading what you have written or you will lose them. You must elevate your readers' interest and hook them emotionally by raising a question for which they want the answer, making captivating statements with well recognized implications, or injecting an element of suspense, comedy, or the deliberate setting of a scene that compels discovery.

You now have the opportunity, when reading the stories at follow, to allow five *TellTale Souls* to lure you in, while seeing to it that when you reach the end of their tales, you'll be glad you took the bait. They make good on their promises to give you, as a reader, what you want.

▶ Alan Rinzler elevates interest by using the emotional hook of raising an introductory question that begs an answer:

Difficult Lessons

~Alan Rinzler

When I was about ten years old, I asked my mother what it was like to be dead. "Do you remember before you were born?" she answered.

"No," I said as we stood outside on the corner backyard porch with open sides and a big pine tree growing through the roof.

"That's what it's like."

Wow! Plain and clear. I knew all I needed to know from Evelyn Rothman Rinzler's point of view as a secular Jewish woman who had been a secret member of the Young Communist League at NYU during the late 1930s, born of Yiddish speaking refugee parents on the Lower East Side, and raised in the Bronx.

My mother taught me some difficult lessons about death and dying. She was always tough, unsentimental, self-centered, and pushy, often embarrassing to have as a mother among my peer group as I was growing up. I eventually separated, had a family of my own, and moved three thousand miles from New Jersey to live in Berkeley, California. But when my father died at only 57, she uprooted herself and moved nearby in Walnut Creek, where she bought her own house with a pool and began a second career as the ombudsperson for Contra Costa County, a big job which gave her a lot of visibility and many people, who were having hard times, to fight for in the courts.

She was very happy, busy, and never very interested in spending time with me or her grandchildren, which was fine with me since I basically feared her and ordinarily regressed to sullen adolescence whenever she was around, which wasn't often. She liked to have us nearby. She'd invite us to her parties, but the boundaries were clear. She was an independent woman. A bundle of energy and good health, she nevertheless got cancer when she was 87 years old and rapidly deteriorated. At this decisive moment, she showed some more class and taught me something about death, again.

Her physical hardships and frailties had reached the point where she couldn't take care of herself, so we researched and located a nearby nursing home which had assisted living and also a medical facility for more medical requirements when needed. She really didn't want to go. This was just awful. The worst thing that could happen. She had to quit her job and give up her beloved home, which she had been living in now for more than twenty-five years. Worst of all, she thought it was too expensive. As a child of the depression, she'd been frugal and withholding financially all her life. "I'm hemorrhaging money," she wailed.

"It's okay Mom. This is what you've been saving for," I told her.

So she packed up, with help from me and my brother, put stuff in storage, and one sunny day we went over to pick her up for the thirty minute drive to the nursing home. She shuffled out slowly toward the car, then stopped for a moment facing away from the house. "I'll never be back. This is it for me. The end." Then without looking back she got into the car slowly and slammed the door herself.

She was right. A month later she was dead.

That's what I remember most about my mother. She was strong, to the point of hard boiled, and self-reliant, separate, not much interested in me or anyone else in the family for that matter, but smart, pragmatic, realistic, mature in that way.

I didn't want more from her, since her critical judgment and tough-minded attitude wasn't always easy to take. It wasn't available, really, and a mixed blessing when it was, in any case. But as far as death and dying is concerned, she's my role model as I get closer to that time myself.

Photo credit to Cheryl Rinzler: Mother and Alan.

Alan Rinzler: "As a book editor (alanrinzler.com) who has worked with authors for more than 47 years, I know I'm no writer. But I'm glad to have had this opportunity to say something about my mom, whom I miss and think about every day with regret and yearning. I wish we had had a better relationship because I loved her dearly, and I'm not sure she knew it. She loved me too, but also wasn't very good at expressing it."

▶ Aileen Bridgewater elevates interest by injecting an element of suspense:

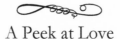

A Peek at Love
~Aileen Bridgewater

As a child I always suspected my mother was married to a British Agent. Mary was a beautiful Irish girl who ran away from home to marry my father because she just couldn't help herself.

Lynn Cook Henriksen

Throughout their marriage they were deeply in love and it showed. We lived on the Isle of Sheppey, a small island in the mouth of the River Thames, sixty miles from London. Sheppey had the doubtful privilege of housing a large important dockyard where the ships were serviced to go back to war. For this reason the island was a target for German bombers. Air raids were frequent. One of my earliest memories was returning home from school one day to find the street where my grandmother lived reduced to rubble.

My suspicions first arose about my parent's involvement in the war effort one night when I was awakened by a loud bang. Rushing to my bedroom window and looking out into the total blackness, it was the time of enforced blackouts, I was surprised to see my mother in the light of the beams of the searchlights crisscrossing the skies. At the front gate she stood motionless, waiting, watching. I was riveted to the window. She stood for long hours it seemed to me as a seven-year-old child. Then my father arrived in the darkness, soaking wet. Inside the house my mother helped him off with his large gum boots and wet clothes. I crept down the stairs and innocently interrupted their hushed chatter. I was surprised by the shocked anxiety on both their faces before I was hurried back to bed. The following morning before I left for school my mother earnestly insisted that I never mention the incident to anyone, ever. Until now I never have.

I went to school on the mainland, and every day my mother walked with me to the railway station. I remember being conscious of her loving anxiety as she hugged and kissed me goodbye when I caught the steam train that carried us across the bridge to the mainland. We were once dive bombed on the way home and thought it quite a joke when the older girls told us to take cover on the dirty railway carriage floor. My mother was at the station to meet me as she was every night. That night her hands were visibly shaking.

My father was in a reserved occupation as a ship's electrician and every few weeks he was sent to guard the bridge. On these occasions my mother would entrust me to pass a note to him as the train stopped just before we made the crossing. One day when her note blew away in the wind, I will always remember the disappointment on my father's face when I had nothing to give him. The next day my mother warned me to be especially careful of

182

the note to be handed over. There was something in her anxious eyes told me it was vital for the war effort that the note reached its destination safely. "Don't give it to anyone else," she repeated. "Make sure it gets to Daddy."

The train stopped at the station before crossing the bridge. I was suddenly overcome with curiosity to read the important secret message she had been so anxious to see not get into the wrong hands. I opened the envelope and peeped inside. I suddenly understood her anxiety over getting it to my father and no one else. In her own rather beautiful handwriting with her favourite fountain pen, she had written, "Jim—I love you....stay safe."

Photo contributed by Lynn Henriksen: Aileen and *TheStoryWoman*.

Aileen Bridgewater: "My career has been meaningful. While hosting "Talk of Hong Kong" for twelve years, I traveled the world-wide to interview people in the news, including Princess Diana, Bob Hope, Sir Edmund Hillary, Fredrick Forsyth, and the Dalai Lama in his Himalayan refuge in India, and many more. In 1994, I was awarded the MBE by Her Majesty Queen Elizabeth for my contribution to broadcasting and the community. But nothing compares to taking the time to bring back memories of my mother so brilliantly. Although my mother died very suddenly while I was still quite young, my life has been greatly inspired by her. She taught me courage, honesty and caring for others. I am deeply grateful for your encouragement, Lynn, to write this story; you brought her back to me. I am grateful, many thanks."

▶ Marvin Wilson elevates interest by making captivating statements with well-recognized implications:

My Mother—The Preacher's Wife
~Marvin D. Wilson

Ellen Elizabeth VanBuskirk Wilson was a preacher's wife by the age of twenty. Dad ministered in the small off-shoot sect of Christianity called the Wesleyan Methodists. Wesleyan Methodists broke away from mainstream Methodists because they felt that Methodists had become too "worldly." The life of a Wesleyan Methodist was a strict religious one. All I remember was all the things you could not do. Can't drink or smoke, can't swear, can't dance, can't sing or listen to songs that are not Christian songs, can't go to the movies, can't wear jewelry, can't wear makeup, can't, can't, can't have any fun, basically.

She lived under intense scrutiny. The religious people were very judgmental. A preacher's wife had to be perfect in every way, the perfect wife, mother, housekeeper, and spiritual example, and from her family the same expectations were exacted. That included the four of us boys, and I, being the oldest, maybe got the brunt of it. I remember seeing church ladies come over to the parsonage and run their fingers across a coffee table to see if there was any dust on it. If there was, they would whisper something to each other. I knew it was derogatory, and about my mother. If I, or any of my brothers,

184

misbehaved in any way, it was an indictment against her and her lack of good parenting.

As a result of this setting in which I grew up, I came to despise religion. I saw nothing but hypocrisy, gossip, back-stabbing, and spirit-less phony play-acting in the whole unhappy, oppressive charade called "the church." I bided my time until I could graduate high school and flew off to college like a bat out of hell, ready to explore and immerse myself in the world I had been shut off from during my youth. I became a Hippie. I got heavy into drugs, sex, and rock and roll.

Why am I writing all of this about me? Because, throughout my entire life, my mother knew and understood what I was going through. Hell, she was going through it, too. She didn't agree with all the "no-isms." She knew that my childhood had been bereft of the normal good, clean fun that other kids had had. But she loved my father. She loved God and the church, too. Although she hoped and wished I had stuck to the faith of my father, she never stopped loving me, caring for me, and praying for me when I went crazy bonkers wild out into the "world." She cried for me, her heart broke apart over me, and she had only faith to hold onto that my soul would be spared. In this, she believed.

It was decades later, in my mid-fifties, that I came back to the Way of Christ ... only the Way I came back to was spiritual, not religious. True freedom, not dogma. Unbridled wild ecstasy in unification with The One, not outdated litanies and strict man-made rules based upon unenlightened literal interpretations of the scriptures. Although she barely recognized my "form" of Christianity, at her age by then, she embraced me and cried tears of joy when I professed my faith to her. "My son has come home. We will be together forever in eternity!"

And that is the spirit, the essence, of my mother. Unending love, non-judgmental compassion, a heart that breaks easily, but never stops pounding with hope, patience beyond measure, faith and belief that "all things work together for the glory of God," and the ability to look beyond circumstances and see the heart of the matter. She is long suffering and able to extract simple pleasure out of the worst that suffering has to offer.

Photo contributed by Marvin: Marvin's spirit shines through.

Marvin Wilson: "Wow! Lynn, thank you! I went through a whole gamut of emotions writing this story; reliving all those memories of frustration and restrained lifestyle, yet all the while feeling this power love—the lifeline thread that held us together. Our family is very tight today—Dad passed ten years ago, but Mom, my brothers, and I love each other very much and get together often. It's great."

▶ Faye Marshall elevates interest by introducing comedic elements:

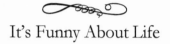

It's Funny About Life

~Faye Marshall

My life started out as a comedy, but I'm not sure whether Mama thought it was so funny at the time. New York City, some street, 1922, ninety miles away from the home in rural Middleton where she and my father lived, it was pouring rain and windy when Mama felt me start to come. Even though she was just seven months along, she knew she had to get to a hospital quick. Before she had felt the first twangs of this labor, she'd walked many blocks from the apartment of the friends she was visiting. Not enough money in her purse for a taxi and the buses just weren't coming. Wet to the skin and brimming with urgency, one hand holding down her navy blue hat, she pulled her billowing blue cape close around her bulging abdomen, stepped into the street, and waved down a fellow driving a pick-up truck. Mama opened her cape, she was showing pretty good for seven months, and said something like, "My baby's on the way. Will you take me to the nearest hospital?" He did. All alone and hitchhiking to a hospital to give birth—that's the kind of spirit Mama had.

It was what she used to call that Hungarian gypsy spirit that filled me and warmed me as a preemie and in all the years to come. From the start, she just plain did what needed to be done without much comment—least ways, no complaining. I was small and had some problems at birth, but Mama saw to it that I got what I needed to thrive. Since her milk didn't come in, two or three times a day she'd go out and buy mother's milk to feed me from an Italian woman who had milk a-plenty.

Mama worked hard in my father's business, but she managed to find personal time for me and for herself. She came from a poor family—poor in dollars, but rich in talent. She instilled in me a love for music and the theater. Mama played the violin from the age of twelve. A couple evenings a week she'd march out the door (my father never approved) to go practice, the violin case in one hand and my hand in the other. As my mother guided the bow gracefully over the strings, I'd do my homework on a makeshift desk or on the floor. My spirit would be filled with the strains of beautiful classical music. Maybe this group wasn't rich or famous, but they could move your soul.

We did a whole lot of singing, dancing, and laughing together, Mama and I. Back then we had only the radio and ourselves for entertainment at home, so we made our own fun, and it was the best fun. Mama had put together a book listing all the songs she knew in various categories, like French, Jewish, romantic, movie, Italian, Hungarian, and on like that. She'd have me look through it to find a title I liked, and then we'd sing and we'd sing and, oh, we'd sing. Eventually I learned all the songs. We did this mostly on car trips. She'd drive, I'd find a song, and we'd sing. Other times, just sitting at the dinner table, we'd only have to look at each other to burst out laughing. We'd laugh until our sides ached or until Papa slammed down his hand, hard and flat, on the tabletop. Then we'd bite the insides of our cheeks to stop our laughter, at least until dinner was over.

Mama, my beautiful mama, died four years ago at the age of ninety-three, and there's still not much I don't tell her. Now we have unspoken communication. She's out of body, which certainly isn't a Jewish way of thinking, but I can't help that I know she's with me. She's here. Her presence is strong.

I sit and look out at a tree in my yard, bursting with whitish-pink, fragrant blossoms, and I feel her. I will always need her.

Faye Marshall: "I'm a communicator, not a writer. My ability to find humor in most everything was instilled in me by my mother. Not a day goes by that I don't think about her, and I keep her violin case in the corner of my room. She not only gave me life, she gave me *life*—I was born with ten physical strikes against me."

▶ Laura McHale Holland elevates interest by the deliberate setting of a scene that compels discovery:

Beside Suicide's Door
~Laura McHale Holland

I was a two-year-old waddling behind my sisters when we came home from a neighbor's Halloween party and found our mother hanging from a basement beam. Several decades later, I wrote a memoir, Reversible Skirt, *about my formative years. Except for the epilogue, the book is written from a child's point of view. My objectives were to give voice to a little girl whose very identity was stolen by events following my mother's demise and to enable readers to experience what it was like to grow up in the shadow of such a tragedy.*

Except for my sisters, I don't know women whose mothers committed suicide, leaving a gaggle of preschoolers behind to grow up with a void where a mother's love should have been. But I'm sure I've met a number of them over the course of my life. I may even be acquainted with such a woman right now.

And therein lies the rub.

We who share this terrible sisterhood tend to keep it hidden. The subject of suicide brings up strong feelings not just for the person who broaches the subject, but also for those listening. To merely tell the truth about my mother means I have to consider not just my own emotions, but also the discomfort it stirs up in those I tell. As a child, this was not something I could handle. Being secretive became habitual.

Which brings me to my silent mother, Mary Agnes, whom I knew throughout my childhood as a black and white photograph on top of my grandfather's bedroom dresser. With her suicide, she slammed an impenetrable door in my face. On this side are questions without answers reverberating endlessly, leaving slivers in my soul, festering too far beneath the surface to reach. Suicide. What a cowardly act, I think, but then I reproach myself for my lack of compassion. I know not the extent of my mother's misery; I cannot judge; she left no note, no clues.

Some wise people say we should be grateful for all the experiences life has brought us—good and bad. I am grateful that my mother gave me life and that she didn't decide to take my sisters and me with her into death. But the fact of her leaving with such force and permanence, no, that's still not cool with me.

And I fear that when my book is published, I'll be doing a meet and greet in a bookstore someday, or visiting a book group, and I'll feel off key as I read a passage or two and answer questions. Why dredge all this up when life in the present is so good? I'll wonder. I hope that when those feelings hit me I'll remember how writing that book set the lost girl inside of me free, and it is her mission to speak to the hearts of those kind enough to listen to the story of one long-ago abandoned child.

Maybe her story will help some future parent discard the thought of suicide should it come to mind during a particularly trying time. And who knows? Maybe on the other side of that door, my mother will be listening too, for, you see, I know the door will never open, but I will forever be longing to connect.

Photo contributed by Laura: Laura at peace within herself.

Laura McHale Holland: "For most of my life, I have been silent on the subject of my mother's suicide. It has seemed impossible to convey with any degree of accuracy what it has been like to have suicide indelibly woven into my core life experiences. I am deeply appreciative that this collection welcomes a diversity broad enough to include an aspect of experience that is for many people taboo."

Note: Laura's memoir, *Reversible Skirt*, was published by Wordforest March 2011.

Were there certain words or images created in the first lines of these stories that made you want to continue reading? If you didn't write them down as you read, please go back over the openings of each story to find which words or phrases excited you and note them now.

> **QUICK WRITE:** Make your opening lines tempting—compelling readers to read on. Let your imagination run free as you generate alternative ways to start your *Mother Memoir*. Write your ideas down quickly—catch hold of inspiring words or phrases that you would not have found if you had forced it or given the matter too much thought.

FILLING OUT YOUR STORY

There are significant ways to add essential elements to your bio-vignette that you may have overlooked. You cannot afford to leave gaping holes in your story for readers to fall into. Yes, you guessed it—they'll be lost forever in Wonderland. So, let's start with the nuts and bolts to make certain your story addresses the five W's, the basic Journalism 101 questions, when you are Filling Out Your Story:

✓ Who ✓ What ✓ When
✓ Where ✓ Why ✓ and How

The often perplexing question, *Why*, has been pondered and poked throughout this book from why it's important to write your *Mother Memoir*, why your mother acted in a certain way, to why stories connect us as nothing else. Now, let's contemplate and connect with *How*, since I listed who, what, when, and where only to remind you of the basics, which you will include in your bio-vignette on your own. For an eye-opening experience that will help you appreciate and further develop various aspects of your mother's character, as well as the overall story, look at how *How* impacts creative nonfiction.

To stimulate the development of your writing, go back through your story and carefully consider the consequences and/or the new slant that will be generated by answering the following types of questions. Please think in terms of questions to ask yourself that are wholly reflective of your unique narrative. These questions are meant to have you supply the meaning of "it," for example, since you are the only one who can provide the context in each instance.

> ➢ How did she do it?
> ➢ How did she know that?
> ➢ How could she?
> ➢ How much did it take?
> ➢ How big a price did she pay?

Don't stop in your search for the clearest and truest sense of the character of your mother—it is often discovered by appropriately and continuously asking *How*. To take this assignment to the next level, mull over *How* the reality of her character may have changed, in your eyes, as a consequence of your journey through the memories of your relationship with her and what has transpired since beginning to write the *Mother Memoir*.

We each see the personality, the character and spirit, and the actions of those around us through light bent by our individual perspective. However, stay open to new perceptions and look at all dimensions of your story from different angles. Your truth will often be very different from someone else's truth, even your sister's, and I will present a good example through two bio-vignettes written by sisters about their mother, after you do a little more musing on the subject. You may be struck more by the differences than by the similarities apparent in various takes on the same woman, event, or experience. Embrace the differences, but trust yourself and your voice in the end.

In asking you to keep an open mind, I am not suggesting you bend your truth to meet another person's truth, just be aware that there are as many ways of seeing as there are of loving people and of understanding their actions. Stick with your truth. Remember that love and understanding do not necessarily go hand in hand, but through writing, the door to understanding begins to open. The following are points and questions to ponder as you fill out our story.

> Is what you thought was black really black or was it deep blue?
> Was what caused her to act a certain way really due to anger or was she acting out of fear?
> Try looking at certain scenes you have in your mind as if you were seeing them for the first time.
> Look at them again from your mother's vantage point.
> Imagine what it must have been like to be in her shoes.
> Try looking at her world through her eyes.
> Look for the lesson in your mother's conscious or unconscious actions.

The two stories below have been written by sisters, both of whom truly loved their mother, but experienced life with her in very different ways.

Comfort Zone

~Liz Herron

Climbing into bed with her just to snuggle. My feet between her warm thighs until each toe was toasty. Soothing words to ease away a bad dream. The feel of sheets fanned across my fevered body when I was ill and her cool hand on my forehead supporting me when I vomited. Memories of my mother are many, but these are the most comforting ones—the thoughts I always come back to.

I can still see her beautiful smile and the laughter in the twinkle of her eyes. Those blue eyes that glanced up from the typewriter over the rims of the reading glasses, her chin tilted down to support the easy smile that welcomed everybody into our home—they were inviting eyes, inquisitive eyes. Mom had a zest for life, an insatiable thirst. She couldn't get enough of it or of the people in it. She asked people questions and listened to their answers without passing judgment, making them feel significant. Our house was the "cool" place to be—the place to hang out. I took all this for granted as if every home was captained by such parents.

As the youngest child of four, and just three-years-old, I recall the feeling of security as I played with my record player, while Mom cooked tapioca in the kitchen. I knew it was she who made sure the slide slid into the kiddie pool and the strawberries grew in our garden. She dressed us in Easter finery with matching bonnets, played a mean game of golf, was a master at bridge, and baked and decorated the best chocolate birthday cakes in the world.

Watching her get dressed-up, helping her zip a cocktail dress, studying her as she applied her makeup and did her hair, she was the most glamorous woman I'd ever set eyes on. She was also my dad's secretary and bookkeeper, and I can still hear her tapping away at the typewriter in the family room as I turned in to bed. The clicking would go on well past midnight while she burned the midnight oil. Yet every morning when I woke the house was picked up, neat as a pin, sack-lunches were made, the dishes were done.

On warm spring days, she'd sometimes let me play hooky, and the two of us would go snow skiing. I was always proud and happy to ride the ski lift with her. In summer she packed endless picnics for boating and water skiing outings. Mom liked to ride on the front of Old Blue, our motor boat; she'd lie on her stomach and straddle one side of the bow, letting me straddle the other side. I loved hanging on to the front light with my hand cupped underneath my mother's—the fresh air, the wind in our faces, the smell of sage, water, and indescribable light combined to make a world where it seemed like nothing could ever go wrong. Mom relished sleeping out in the screened-in porch at our summer cabin, where she could hear the insect sounds of the night, see the stars of the universe, and catch the first glimpse of the morning light as the sun greeted a new day.

We were always late for church on Sundays, and Mom would sometimes fall asleep—her only respite from the all-inclusive motherhood—and snore slightly, or jerk, or sneeze her odd little squeal. I was terribly embarrassed until I realized Mom would be lovingly holding my hand during the entire service. Then I knew her church napping didn't matter.

As I grow older and limp along in her footsteps, I stand in awe of all that she accomplished. And I wonder how she did it all. It must have been the magic fairies or perhaps the wee leprechauns helping her pull it off. Today, with a nanny and cleaning woman and only one child—my four-year-old Katie—I can only marvel at my mother's grace.

I like to think that Mom's soul merged with Katie's soul and she lives again. Katie will never know my mother in the flesh, but my mother will visit her every time I hold Katie's forehead when she's sick and when she snuggles her feet between my thighs in the mornings after she crawls in bed with me. Grandma Beth will be there when I brush Katie's hair, rub her tummy, decorate her homemade birthday cakes, and she'll be with us in our boat when I wrap my arm around Katie and the wind rushes through our hair.

My mother lives inside me; she is with me every day. I will carry her with me till the day I die. She was a mother unlike any other mother in the world and she was a mother like every other mother in the world.

Liz Herron: "Even though I'm a dentist, actress, wife, and mother, I feel like the "little sister" who wonders what she'll do when she grows up. My soul is keenly aware of what I have and have not accomplished, and I see negativity and worry needs to be replaced with exercise and laughter. Life is so short, I must travel quickly."

Photo courtesy of the Christy and Liz: Our mother.

Comfort Zone is an appropriate title for how Liz viewed life with her mother. Her sister, Christy, coping with *An Enigma*, craved to know and understand her mother on a deeper level and more openly:

An Enigma

~Christy D'Ambrosio

I have persistently procrastinated in writing this story rather than be disloyal or do anything to dishonor the memory of a wonderful woman who was my mother. Wonderful—did I use that word because I should, or because many others, including my daughters, saw my mother as wonderful? Or was it because I wish she might have been such a mother to me?

My mother died in my arms as I told her how beautiful she was, what a wonderful woman and mother she had been, Why I, a kindergarten through-twelfth-grade Catholic school girl, didn't revert to an Act of Contrition, I'll never know. But these words I uttered—the last words she would hear on earth— seemed to hold for her some meaning.

I, the eldest of her four children, had sought to avoid this moment of death. Yet it was I who grew from this feared last moment of responsibility. In the end, it was my privilege.

I sat alone outside in the spring evening a few hours after she was gone and reflected on this mother of mine. One thought repeatedly bumped through my mind, "I didn't ever know her." I didn't. She will remain an enigma to me, I know I could have tried harder, especially in the later years, to get beyond her facade, but I didn't. Why? After all, I have an advanced degree in psychology. I am a marriage and family therapist with a successful private practice. I should have been able to "crack her open" even just a little. But it wasn't to be.

Yes, she did everything "right" for her children. As the world saw her, my mother was a prime example of the perfect mother of the 1940s and 50s—our dresses were perfectly ironed, our hair shone with curls and light; we had the best ballet teachers and college educations. She was a lady of the old school and a lady didn't air her dirty laundry—which meant past experiences were left in the past and anything emotional was not to be discussed. So our relationship was polite, careful, frustrating. In the end, I was left with unfulfilled wishes. As a custodial mother, I give her an A. But I really wanted a Mom.

Christy D'Ambrosio: "I think my mother loved me, but I don't think she liked me. When she found herself pregnant with me, it was a difficult time for her. She had been a spoiled child and a queen bee, so she heaped too much responsibility on me as my brother and sisters came along. In the final analysis, I believe she resented me, and I grew to resent her."

What are the truths in your story that leave a tang? Can you imagine there may be a way to refocus the lens through which you view you mother?

REVISIT what you have written from an altogether different vantage point, by looking at every aspect of your bio-vignette through different shades of light and focus.

CREATING THE SCENE WITH ESSENTIAL ENERGY

Life's energy is the soul of the *Mother Memoir*. Scientists have concluded that energy can neither be created nor destroyed, but it can change from one form to another. At this point, you have located stored energy from memories, and, through writing, you are now transforming that vital force into a story that has immeasurable meaning for you. Think about the energy you feel when engaging with your mother's spirit as you reflect and write, and then ask yourself if you have effectively transferred that force of life to the written page.

As I began collecting stories from *TellTale Souls*, I immediately felt a basic, essential energy emanating from the intimate slices of life contained in their true tales. The spirit of the unassuming characters in each story—the mothers portrayed and the daughters and sons writing—took on organic form, slid in under my skin and flowed into my soul, personal energy connecting me to them. I imagine you feel the same as you read the stories throughout this book. *TellTale Soul* Marlene remembers her grandmother's energy:

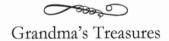

Grandma's Treasures

~Marlene Mason

"*I'm surrounded by man energy!*" *Grabbing the big straw broom, I flounce at dirt embedded in deep-grooved floors, at cobwebs interlaced in rough-cut log walls, swipe at spiders scurrying to the bare rafters. I slam wood into the old woodstove, banging its leaden door, striking a match against its pitted face. Water from the rough-handled pump rushes into the cast iron pot…everything is rough, rough, rough! No doors on the rooms, no privacy, no grace…ah, except there! I can see it in my granddaughter's face.*

Her soft little hand clasped in mine, out into the woods we escape; our pounding feet leaving puffs of dust hanging in the still air. Stopping, we catch our breath. I watch as she squats as only small children do, knees wide, elbows braced, hands clasped; she is mesmerized by the rollie-pollie bug she's spotted on the ground.

She giggles her tiny girl laugh as we lay side by side on the needled carpet. Gazing up at the fern forest above our heads, I say, "Let's make ourselves small! We can be caterpillars." I see the journey begin in her eyes. "Make yourself small, small, small. Imagine what a little bug sees…how big everything would be. Here we go!" As we begin to shrink, I describe for her how it would be, to be ever so small. As she looks up at me, I laugh…she knows.

We climb over pine needle logs, between rock mountains and gaze up at the towering green above. "It's a very long climb. Hold on tight." I can smell the damp earth, the taste of dirt in my mouth. She tells me her tummy is tickled by the fern hairs covering the stalk and I tell her mine is too by the bumpy spores out under the fronds and that I'm dizzy from hanging upside-down. We crawl and we crawl then I point down to the girl and her grandmother lying far below on the ground.

We make our way back; our edges all soft and blurred. With bug-smiles still upon our faces, we pass from "out there" to "in here"; neither so different now. We split the peas from their smooth pods, slip them into the rolling water; her fingers butterfly wings against mine.

I remember this day as one of the happiest of my childhood. I watch as her angular lines relax into soft curves, her voice moving from sharp to low. I feel her rough hands holding mine, and the two of us dissolving to the ground.

My grandmother took me with her as she traversed the universe, taking us beyond our bodies, expanding into the dark night. She taught me to use the stars as stepping stones to leap across the sky. I galloped with her on tree-horses through plains of Indian Territory and walked on the beaches of

Hawaii with her rhododendron leis in my hair. I've looked and found fairies dancing in forest glens, and counted unicorns leaping over the moon as she lay beside me so I didn't travel alone. And I've stomped down dirt roads, trailing released anger in my wake as she taught me, by example, to do.

I think now of the house in the coastal forest, just outside Fort Bragg, California, she and my grandfather built with trees cleared from the land. I remember the redwood trees, giants touching the skies. I remember the don't-walk-barefoot weathered porch and the hated outhouse I feared, sure I'd fall in and never be found. I remember the dangerous-for-children-do-not-touch old wood-fueled cook stove, the freeze-your-hands well water pumped in the kitchen sink, and the I-can't-lift-it iron pots she slung around. I remember sweet-peas, carnations, and my grandmother's favorite gladiolas; toast with butter, sugar, and cinnamon beside bittersweet hot cocoa; the smell of wood smoke in our hair.

I remember my silent grandfather, a salmon fisherman, who brought home, for grandmother to cook for us in her iron frying pan, be-careful-of-the-bones fish I was afraid to eat, along with an occasional mysterious net-encased bubble of glass he called a float, though I never saw them on the water. And I remember my three uncles and my father arguing, arguing, arguing—so different from my grandmother's grace filled energy and way of working with life.

I remember the last time I saw my grandmother, several days after she died, and after I'd seen the woman lying in the coffin they said was her. I know they lied because she came to me later, like morning mist on sea, saying her gentle "Good-bye." They all said I was dreaming, but I know my grandmother's smile.

My grandmother lives in the lush forest of my memory, moving amid the fog-drenched air, dancing with fairies, talking with bugs, traveling in lightning bolts across the sky, ever reminding me how much I am loved.

Photo Contributed by Marlene: Grandmother Dora Stead.

Marlene Mason: "Writing this story about my grandmother was a profound experience for me. Not only did my grandmother's spirit come to life within me as I wrote, my spirit was infused with the passion, joy and unbound excitement to travel in time and space to converse with the many spirits who've touched my life over the years and to invite them to be heard and remembered."

Marlene's bio-vignette is bursting with energetic imagination, as are the following three poems. It was interesting to me that three women in their twenties wrote their *Mother Memoirs* in verse with passion and emotion. Jennifer's poem is one of only two telling tales in the collection written in second person—she is speaking directly to her mother.

Mother Nurture

~Jennifer Bruno

Mother
You are stories of squirrels in the tree outside my window
Delight in new fallen snow on Christmas Day, thunderstorms
One bite out of a pb&j

You are kisses on boo-boos
A laugh in the middle of tears
Comforting silence in times of sorrow

You are the wish that came true on a falling star
A perfect crayon coloring (always within the lines)
The only acceptable playmate for Barbie

You are blueberries and cottage cheese on toast
Surprise love notes in backpacks
The cure for any sickness, including a broken heart

You are lambies singing children to sleep
Homemade apple pie
Freshly painted pinkred toenail polish

You are the sweet smell of baby Samantha
Hand-stitched teddy bear nightgowns
Quilted letters of your daughters' names

You are driving permits and frozen yogurt
Easter dresses and daffodils
"I Love You" in sign language

You are dedication and honesty
The apology after anger
Best friend and confidant for life

You are the love of sisters
Naked Ladies in the summertime
A giggle at your own expense

You are the bells of Santa Claus, a gift in my slipper
Knitting sweaters with my brother
The "fleur" in French

You are the face of pride at graduation
Pure joy at my wedding
Freedom and independence

You are the eyes of your mother
The smile of your grandmother
The bond of sisterhood

You are my mother
You are within me
In my body, in my soul
Forever

Photo contributed by Jennifer: My daughter, Kate, and I.

Jennifer Bruno: "It's so important to remember all the little things in life that actually aren't little things at all. They come together to make a relationship strong and intimate. I love you Mom for all the connections I couldn't do without."

Lynn Cook Henriksen

She's Mine

~Samantha Furgason

They all wish she was theirs
but she's not
she's mine

my mother

makes art
from animal bones
and
fish bodies

buys prepackaged meat
at the grocery store
someone else
skins
cleans
and cuts
then
"it is no longer meat"
she says

she predicts the future
she can tell you what will happen
100% accurately

my mother finds intricate qualities
in centipedes

in my mother's house
there are no good snacks

only tofu
old blue corn chips

my mother likes everyone
and
everyone
loves my mother

a friend says
that she is
a wonderful
sick and twisted
storehouse of knowledge

my mother had a
weakness
for my father
i
have a
weakness
for my father

my mother
made my brother

when she needs something
or
tries to prove a point
her voice
raises
one octave

she cries
when you do something

Lynn Cook Henriksen

nice for her

my mother loves
me

thunder feeds her soul

she will live to be 93
and famous

my mother sacrifices
always gets the
broken
or
small
portion

she would lend me 10
if she had 5

eats
standing up
after everyone else
is through

my mother doesn't smoke
but has for 40 years
but yesterday was the last time
really

i said
one
two
three

and jumped on my mother's back
every day
till i was 20

my mother will never
be stuck in a nursing home
i'll make sure
my brother takes good care of her

they all wish she was theirs
but she's not
she's mine
my mother

Photo contributed by Samantha: My son, Tien, and I.

Samantha Ferguson: "As a baby, my mother carried me from window to window during electrical storms saying, "Oooooh, wonderful," at each crash of thunder. Story of my life. I am not fearful. When life presents me with a loud crash, my essence reminds me, 'Oooooh, wonderful.'"
www.artworkinternational.com

Both Samantha, in the previous poem, and Dominique, in the following poem, demonstrated fierce ownership of their mothers. And all three of the women spanned long periods of time in their relationships with their mothers through their poetic verses.

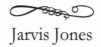

Jarvis Jones

~Dominique Crawley

Jarvis Jones. The super-poised, elegant and graceful, reserved—yet feisty, completely distinguished mother of mine.

Jarvis Jones. A woman so strong and resilient she was given a man's first name. Successful entrepreneur, who put mustard greens and hot water corn bread on the table by way of her creativity.

Jarvis Jones. Eternally wealthy, even with her food stamps buried deep down in her purse. Dignified and proud as she tells you that she only used them for three months.

Jarvis Jones. Quiet as she seethes with power and confidence. Bold enough to survive off her eye for beauty and quick mind. She's a Jones— we're all just trying to keep up with her.

Jarvis Jones the critic. "Keep practicing your "Js" until they look like this," she critiques my beginner's cursive. Forever striving for perfection and excellence—she is determined. Articles in the paper praise her for her unique style—she is extraordinary.

She is my mother.

A day in the life of Jarvis Jones. "Come on Nique, let's go." Our caramel brown, but far from sweet, 1980 Mercury hums as we travel through Marin County, draping the wealthiest of wives in original haute couture pieces. Her work is spectacular.

Raw silk pant suits, hand painted silk blouses, with the brightest of hues, splashing about the fabric—she only works with the best. She is my mother.

I watch her frown her eyes tight as she delicately places pins here and there, careful not to prick her human canvas. "Stop frowning your face or you'll end up with wrinkles like these." She points to her forehead as I relax my eyes.

She engages in pleasant and friendly chatter with her client. "Oh Jarvis, this is lovely. I'll need another piece for the Grammy's." She smiles, "For you I have the perfect design. You'll be second to no one on the red carpet." The epitome of professionalism and class—she is talented. Keeps her clients coming back—they love her.

She is my mother.

Always listening and supporting. She is my one-woman cheerleading squad. Forever encouraging and inspiring. "If anybody else can do it—you can too!"

She is my mother.

Made me feel like the most important person in the world. She raised me. "It's a good thing you got your common sense from me."

She's my greatest adviser and closest confidant. She's always right— she's my best friend. She's the best grandmother. Ruins my child, but she taught me right.

Jarvis Jones. Southern belle, heart of gold, patient and cool, writing letters to the principal of the school, bringing homemade butter pecan cake straight from the oven to the bake sale.

She's my mother.

Jarvis Jones. Majestic and regal in her own right. A strong voice at the PTA meeting, and a graceful hand stitching together costumes for our ballet company's performance.

She was there for me.

"Dog girl, you got big! Now what you want me to cook?" My pregnant belly growls remembering Mama's cooking. "I want some dressing. And some greens. And some sweet potatoes."

She was there.

The springtime brought my mother to Washington, DC, and together we watched her grandson make his debut. She loves him, holds him close, stares at his face as she gently bounces. She watches me. "Be careful with him!" As I hoist him up in a motherly huff.

More greens, African chicken, black-eyed peas—she pampers me. She stays with me. I learn to be a mother with my mother. She was by my side. She silently teaches me. She holds my baby. She's soft. She smiles.

Jarvis Jones. Obama's face on her chest as she chills in the Bahamas sipping on coconut rum—she is fabulous. Short red 'fro, high cheek bones, and full lips. She's beautiful.

She's my mother. I love her.

Photo complements of Dominique: My son, Aasani, and I.

Dominique Crawley: "True satisfaction would come from my son deeming me to be half as good a mother as Jarvis Jones."

The bottom line is that incredible energy is created by the weaving of emotional threads of the past throughout your bio-vignette. It is energy that piques interest, and it is interest that makes a story compelling. So far you have had a look at what energy is as a life force, and, from the beginning of this book, you have read story examples with scenes expressing it through the complete range of feelings and emotions, from laughter to sadness and everything in between. In memoir, you become aware of scene as the setting for the theme of your story, the backdrop for the incident(s) you are describing in which your mother plays the leading role—she is seen in the scene.

Your bio-vignette may be one scene only, a few at most, because you're writing a mini-memoir. But your scene is every bit as important as a memoir filled with hundreds of scenes, in fact, what you are writing is even more important because it stands alone, practically as one thought in and of itself, and it must tell a complete and inspiring story in one vibrant swoop. What could be better than to use your ever-present senses to build an energetic scene? Any time you can size up a scene by using your senses you will call into being rich qualities to add dimension to your characters and to the story in general. Stories need a scene or scenes, and a scene need sensory hooks. Within a scene, all of your senses are alert, some more than others; although, you may not be consciously aware of what they register until you make a conscious effort to be more sensitive to them.

It makes good sense to ask yourself the following questions when contemplating a scene at any moment in time:

> ➢ What is there to SEE beyond the immediate image in my mind? What color are the silky ribbons mom braided into my hair, as I twisted my head angrily away when she accidentally pulled one strand too tight?
> ➢ What is there to SMELL in the scene I have in mind? What was that pungent odor captured in the thick August air at the campsite?
> ➢ What is there to HEAR in the background of this scene? Do I hear her laughter and become reminded of her animated face glowing, eyes twinkling, and wrinkles crinkling?
> ➢ What is there to TOUCH in this scene, and how does it feel? Are the boards of the porch underneath my bare feet rough and dry or damp and slippery?
> ➢ What does this scene or anything in it TASTE like? Does the whole place taste like anger after an outburst? If so,

how would I describe the taste of anger?

➢ What is there to INTUIT about this scene? Does my sixth sense tell me the smile on her face is nothing but a façade?

Now I want you to actualize events or moments in time through the senses of your characters. Tricky? Not doable? Not really. Just try it. You will be amazed at how much closer you'll get to the heart of your characters once you begin to imagine what they see, hear, taste, touch, and smell. Also, begin to grasp what you think they intuitively may have gleaned from experiences you're writing about that included them. Stand in their shoes, but this time slide into their skin as well. Doing this will give you more insight into your mother, for example, but it won't reveal her truths. No matter how close you are to anyone, her truths can only be known to her, just as your truths can only be realized by you, but it does provide a valuable means to better understanding her as an individual unto herself. *TellTale Soul* Dan does an excellent job, while dodging arrows, becoming conscious of his mother's plight in this thoughtful true story:

The Blues

~Dan O'Neill

Being born the third of five (and eventually six children), I was the observer. I think a position description was stapled to my birth certificate at the hospital. The laughter left our home early in my childhood. As my father's failing business and drinking became more of an obsessive terror, the laughter bled away, increasing in flow with each new disappointment, assault, or enforced silence. I watched my mother's heart break. Her cheeks grew thin and her color paled as if her soul had been bled. Dresses became housecoats, her singing stopped.

The worse things became, the more she ironed her blue starch on everything. It was her escape, the ironing board and the radio. Like a matriarchal elephant imprisoned, she had a nervous, deliberate rocking, dreaming of how it should be, but unable to act.

One morning she sent me to the corner grocer for bread, "The day-old bread, it's just as good and will save us some money." She handed me a five-dollar bill from her cache of what little money she was able to secret away. I skipped along to the grocer, got the bread and ran home, dodging Indian arrows, enemy soldiers' bullets, and fighter planes.

When I arrived home, I put the bread in the kitchen and went to Mom's ironing corner to give her the change. As I stood before her I reached into my pocket, but there was nothing there, just the bottom of my pocket. Her whole aspect changed. I searched all my pockets, the bag that held the bread, then meticulously every step of the way to and from the grocer for what seemed like hours. There were no bullets or arrows to dodge now, just the terrible emptiness of having disappointed her.

I remember her asking me, "How could you be so careless." When I looked up at her, it wasn't an angry scowl that met my eyes, but fear— moreover, panic. Her blue eyes drained of color, tears welled in them. The constant head-to-toe motion that went with ironing had ceased, but she clung to that iron as if it packed an even more powerful hope for mercy and salvation than the ever-present blue plastic rosary in her housecoat pocket.

Dan O'Neill: "Writing this story gave a ghost some substance, and through writing it, I discovered that my strength came from my mother."

I think it is important to note that the sense of smell is one of the most powerful senses we can use when we are tapping memory or when we are describing people and places, because smell is tied most closely with our limbic system, which is the primary area in the brain that has to do with memory and our emotions, including our response to pain and pleasure. I am sure you can recall many times throughout your life when the nostalgic smell of something instantly transported you to a place where the grass was newly mown, the bread was baking, the smell of fire was paralyzing, the diaper needed changing, the salt air was tantalizing, or the whiff of her signature perfume brought you joy and sadness rolled into one. What does fear, love, longing, anger smell like to you? Use all of your senses creatively and in combination to add layers and complexity to a scene.

To build a scene, the technique of overstating actions is often used in creative writing. Most of us are guilty of occasionally overstating incidents to get our points across in conversation, or we overstate action due to how powerfully we reacted to someone or something on an emotional level. Comedians thrive on exaggerating scenes to get laughs. Although I don't believe it has a place in a finished memoir, this technique can be useful when ferreting out memories and jotting down impressions to evoke feelings and emotions. Have some fun toying around with this literary device as you develop a scene, but, in the end, stick to the truth—truth can be stranger than fiction.

When the feelings or attitudes of your characters change within the scenes of your story, the tone or tempo of your writing must show this shift in mood. These shifts in tempo are called beats. Beats move stories along, and they can be thought of as turning points or triggers that send characters into action, while requiring a response from the reader. Beats can be as benign as an insinuation or a hint toward some physical action, or they may show a change in emotions, even something puzzling or mysterious that must be ferreted out to change the current mood or activity of your character or storyline. Beats add necessary conflict and tension, essential energy, to the narrative. In the following story, a mix of prose and poetry, we find *TellTale Soul* Linda and her sister standing at their mother's bedside as an emotional storm rages and beats change with the rhythm of passion.

She's Gone

~Linda Branson Smith

She's gone.
Restless, she knew that it was time for her to go.
"A big storm is coming," she said,
and we agreed,
knowing that we would be shaken to our foundations
by the forces that would come.

Clinging to each other,
drawn to the eye of the storm,
we stared, amazed by the energies that raged
within us and around us.

Constantly moving,
she pulled us and pushed us,
eyes searching for the exit and the entrance
open only to her.

Clumsily we tried to help,
to let her go;
"It's okay, Mama," we told her,
as our ears filled with the echoes
of our unspoken pleas for her to stay,
howling like the silent wind
that swept through the room.

As the storm quieted,
she slipped away

and we, having ridden the storm,
walked into the warm night
and were greeted by the moon.

I always knew she would wait to die until I was there with her. When I walked into her hospital room, I could feel a change in the energy and knew that she was starting to die. The sky was cloudless, but she looked outside and said, "A storm is coming."

I was her baby, the last of six children, born when she was forty-two. I had just had my forty-second birthday when she died. Being with her for the next day and a half, watching her make the transition, I saw her die with grace. I watched her change, the wrinkles disappearing from her face, her skin becoming translucent. She was so beautiful. I never wanted to hold onto someone as much as I did then, but I knew the only thing I could do for her was to let her go.

She's been gone over six years now, and I still think about calling her on the phone. Instead, I just talk to her whenever I need to, and I believe she hears me.

Photo contributed by Linda: My mother and I.

Linda Branson Smith: "My mother's death was a turning point where I began singing blues & jazz for real, because I realized you have to put yourself out there by simply stating what you are down deep inside—it's my passion and very healing. This photograph was taken about a year and a half before she passed."

Share your feelings and your journey by talking to friends and family about the emotional truths that have come up for you, but only if it feels right. And then . . .

WRITE: Comprehensively rework the scene(s) of your bio-vignette to enliven it by actively using all of your senses to infuse the story with life's energy. Listen to the rhythm of your beat changes. Visualize the impression (negative or positive) overstating action makes. Write, rework, and write some more.

WORKING WITH THE *ZEITGEIST* AND BACKSTORY

Your story is all about a time—a moment in time. But what time was it? What were the prevailing ideas and the spirit of the time, the *Zeitgeist,* which will hold your memoir in place? Many of you may have already included some aspects of the "times" in your story, but if you haven't, provide a little hint now of the era in which the event or incident takes place so that it will make more sense to you and to the reader.

To successfully write memoir, you need to bring the reader into the scene. In order to do this, it is essential you look at each place and period of time as having a personality uniquely its own. The *Zeitgeist* will have enormously influenced the hearts and minds and actions of your characters. Adding the flavor of the times to your story provides depth and color, but it also acts as a frame of reference as your readers get comfortable with the actions of your characters.

Adding a significant date here and there, naming a world leader, mentioning a famous song, a movie, or a popular dance step of the time, noting a war or the make of an automobile will all create the back-drop for your memoir. Although, keep this in mind, when you add new elements for clarity and better perception, they must meld seamlessly with your story.

In combination with the *Zeitgeist,* let's look into the backstory which you may have intuitively used without giving it a second thought. What backstory amounts to is looking at the history, if it is available, of the person now, not the times, who you have chosen to write about; what makes her who she is up to the time in which your story takes place? Actors also use this device to "get into" their characters—get under their skin, so to speak, so they can better play a role in a stage play or movie. The backstory can also incorporate other essentials that lie beneath the surface of the story itself; those things leading up to the event that left a lasting impression on you.

I bring this to your attention because locating the backstory, the information behind the woman or incident, lets you examine more deeply the "mother mystery": Who is she—what makes her tick? In so short a story as your bio-vignette, using what you have learned of her as an individual and the events framing her life need not necessarily be woven into your memoir, but it will affect your consciousness and, therefore, your writing. The result will lend a greater appreciation and acceptance of her situation. After thinking critically about the forces that coincided to shape your mother's character and telling your truths in the process of writing the *Mother Memoir*, you will be all the wiser for the effort.

WRITE: Make quick notes initially, which may amount to only a word or two, denoting simple impressions of the facts, the backstory, surrounding your mother through the signs of her time. After you have made these quick notes, take time to expand and explore each impression, both critically and intuitively.

TellTale Soul Will explored his past grief through tearful eyes, until he was finally able to successfully come to grips with "a young boy alone in sorrow." By looking at his relationship with his mother from a new vantage point, he found lessons of love and a better understanding of the complex and painful emotions that had held him captive for decades. Will's story fully embodies the aspects of energy, scene building, backstory, and intuitive thinking we have covered throughout Act Four.

My Dream

~Will Meecham

Perhaps it was the last time I saw her.

We lived in a remodeled house on Woodcrest, with freshly painted clapboard siding, and a lawn that always looked like it needed mowing. Since our life there lasted less than a year, I surprise myself by remembering the name of the street. Lined by lookalike houses placed as regularly as railroad cars, Woodcrest had nothing to distinguish it from countless other suburban streets around Detroit. My mother's father had built a handful of those postwar subdivisions, so with a bit of effort he had his construction company redesign our little gray tract house. As a result, it differed from all the others, with two extra bedrooms and a garage converted into a playroom. But if you looked at the house from the street, it still appeared identical to the rest. God forbid we look different from the neighbors. My mother had enough trouble as the only divorcee on the block. This was 1964, and broken families still scandalized the neighborhood.

~~~

I had just climbed the stairs to find my mom opening my dresser drawers and placing neatly folded clothing into a slightly tattered brown and tan suitcase. As my mother added in some rolled up socks and my favorite toy fighter jet, I knew she was preparing me for yet another sleepover with my grandparents. I stopped and stared at her and began the process of boiling into a tantrum. She didn't look surprised when I started trembling with fury; everyone was used to my quick temper. I shrieked, whined, and stamped my feet. "I don't want to go! Don't make me go! I want to stay with you!" Perhaps because she wore an unfamiliar facial expression, as if resigned to eternal grief, I felt more fear of being apart from her than ever before. She grasped my arms and hugged me firmly against her breasts. Her eyes might have been wet with tears.

They say she received over thirty treatments with electroshocks in the course of her many hospitalizations. Sometimes when she left my mother seemed far away, shoulders and head huddled forward, arms wrapped around her torso. Her demeanor this time felt different. Her arms, at once both firm and tender, warmed me through to my boyish frame, and I could feel the rise and fall of her chest as she pulled me close. She was the most beautiful woman I knew, and I gradually melted into her embrace. A six-year-old boy adores his mother with a soul-saturating passion that he tries to rediscover for the rest of his life.

"You don't want Grandma and Grandpa to think you don't love them, do you?" I remember her exact words, and I can almost hear her voice soothing me like a mourning dove's song. She sounded tender and sorrowful, radiant with affection, but also as if she were leaning out a train's window, the details of her face fading as a coal-colored and implacable engine tugged her away from me, gathering speed.

I calmed. Her touch and her words had that effect on me. Beyond the innate responses of motherhood, she believed love should be profuse and resilient, no matter how furious, disappointed or despairing someone felt. I had been taught to return to love quickly, and I knew my grandparents deserved my affection. My attitude became pliant, and I let her finish packing flannel pajamas and wool socks while I sat on the bed and watched. My cheeks were damp, my eyes puffy from quiet sobs.

It might have been the last time I saw her.

~~~

"You're lying! It's not true! Shut UP!" This tantrum went on and on. We were gathered in the tiny living room of my father's mother, which always seemed crowded to me. The carpeted floor was nearly obliterated by overstuffed furniture upholstered with exuberant floral prints, but faded into a dusty and pinkish pastel. Not long before, while scrambling fast across the carpet on my hands and knees, I had impaled my index finger with one of my grandmother's sewing needles. My father had required pliers to pull it out because, as he told me, it had penetrated all the way to the bone. For some reason, I had barely cried.

Now, however, I did not hold back my tears. I felt a rage explode inside me that was unlike any prior outburst. I shook so severely I could barely stand. Tears burned down my cheeks like drops of hot oil. My entire mind, *body, and heart screamed for my mother's embrace, but it did not come.*

The adults let me cry. They were too shattered themselves to provide comfort. I retreated into a corner and sat down, hugging my knees and regressing to sucking my thumb. When my father phoned from Minnesota I could barely whisper to him. "Have Grandma make you some warm milk," he said. Leave it to my dad to suggest drinking a liquid to drown my grief.

~~~

She loved my father too much. After the divorce her faith in the redemptive power of affection and kindness must have been tested. She never gave up on it, despite the feelings of betrayal and jealousy that consumed her. When he married his mistress, her wounded psyche crumbled like dry clay. "God, just let me die!" When I heard her pleading, I would enter her room to visit her as she lay sobbing in her single bed, the air layered with a stale cloud of cigarette smoke. I would sit next to her, fascinated by the dust motes drifting in the thin shafts of sunlight squeezing between the pulled curtains.

Despite her torment, and even after the nuclear battles that preceded the divorce, she never said an unkind word to me about my father. She forgave him. She forgave him completely even though she was limping through life with a fractured heart, saddled with two needy children, facing piles of bills on the chrome and Formica kitchen table, and living in a house owned by her mother.

As much as anyone ever has, she was dying of a broken heart. But when I fell off my bicycle she still wiped my tears with an embroidered handkerchief, and left a trace of lipstick on my forehead.

~~~

Part of me refused to believe that my mom would never come for me. I remained stranded in that living room where they told me she had died. I sat sobbing in the corner, waiting for my mother to gather me back into her arms. I wanted to feel safe again.

I don't know when I finally believed her death, or when I gave up and accepted she would never come back. It might not have been until I was ten. Or maybe a small part of me still clings to the prayer that she will return, smiling at last. Perhaps my heart keeps watch for her, expecting to see her unchanged, thirty-six and lovely, the face of a goddess leaning down to kiss my forehead as I lay on my pillow. "Hush," she would say, "it was only a dream."

Will Meecham: "At fifty years old, on disability, and looking back at a surgical career cut short by arthritis and a mental illness largely resulting from childhood losses, I sometimes blame my mother for giving in to her depression and leaving me adrift. After the bio-vignette about my mom flowed out of me, as if the memories had been dammed up for years, I felt liberated. I've spent a great many years ducking the fact that I was held down by such an anchor of pain about the woman who gave birth to me. At last I found myself able to appreciate her lesson that love is the most important force in the world. I realized that she was the one who guided me to offer love to all, to the best of my ability. This project brought much buried sorrow to the surface and it has given me the strength to pick up that burden and embrace it as my mother's final gift."

Will's story provides another fine example of the incomparable value in writing *Mother Memoir*. It is my sincere belief that you'll appreciate the significance found in all of the heartfelt stories that are part and parcel of this guidebook, and that you'll do your part to keep the *Mother Memoir* vibrant by looking at your mother from the inside out.

As I began to pull together the elements of this book on how to tap memory and write memoir, I realized I had dozens of real-people, real-life stories that really must be woven throughout, in just the right places, to illustrate my guiding points to writers. After all, I considered the fact that when teaching and presenting the *TellTale Souls* writing method in person, people find the story examples invaluable to the learning process. They tell me listening to or reading other people's short, true tales helps them give shape to the bio-vignettes they are forming into personal stories to keep mothers' spirits alive. In the end, that was how this book took final shape as it was refined into a creative writing tool. It came together beautifully like pieces to a puzzle. In the final section of Act Four, you have the opportunity to shape and refine your bio-vignette in much the same way—using more creative ideas to make your work as powerful as you can make it. The giant jig-saw puzzle *TellTale Souls* have begun will not be complete without your story...

SHAPING AND REFINING

In Act Three I suggested using your imagination as poetic license to help your story take shape. You could substitute the words "artistic" and "creative" for "poetic" when thinking about this license to permit yourself to fill the gaps in fragmentary memories. Some folks call artistic license a distortion of facts, even deception. I call it the freedom to choose to act creatively when writing personal narrative. To be sure, memory itself is a form of fabrication—you are reconstructing the images of people and events, although, you are doing so with no interest to deceive. The aim and intent of the *Mother Memoir* is to be authentic and to tell the truth as you see it. You are constructing a memoir from the fabric of your mind, where, in order to shape your story, form it into a complete narrative, you may unite images from different events stored in memory. Remember, make sure the incidents and characteristics you are recalling are real and belong in the story as you build it.

As you continue to shape and refine your story, try using a special blend of fine tuning and finishing touches. Add these *fine touches* by bringing together the notes and details you gathered from the wide range of writing exercises you worked on over the course of this guidebook. Pay particular attention to your feelings and emotions, the fine points of your relationship with your mother, and the essential characteristics of her being. Then *show* these specific details by making them apparent as you describe her through *action*. Remember to give yourself permission to use artistic license as you refine your bio-vignette.

The following are questions to consider on several fronts when shaping your story. From the ideas generated in this list, you'll think of other questions, pointedly specific to your circumstances, to ask yourself:

➤ Is her hair blonde or strawberry-blonde?
➤ Were her actions the result of anger or was she acting out of deep concern?
➤ What do aspects of this scene look like from her point of view?
➤ What does it feel like to be in her shoes? In her skin?
➤ If I could go back and look at this scene for the first time, would it be different from the memory I've carried around with me for 10 years, maybe 50 years?

Think about the countless possibilities you have to combine description with action. For example, you could say, "My mother has blonde hair." Or you could say, "She absently brushed strawberry blonde strands from her forehead and bit her lip as she struggled to take in the news I just gave her." Give your mother something to do in her role as leading lady so that she shows up in a scene as a living, breathing character, rather than flat as a photograph. Action reigns supreme.

Another way to improve your story is to reexamine the overall tone and voice carrying the story. Also ask yourself if your mother's voice rings true. In Act Two, we went over the reasons why it works to write like you talk—and your characters talk. This amounts to the most honest and interesting form of communication. The same holds true when you write dialogue or quote someone. Let the words reverberate in your head—do the words match the speaker—until what you have on paper is an authentic representation of each person's voice. Anchor characters to scenes using words and actions that fit like a glove.

Ask yourself:

> ➤ Are the speech and mannerisms of the characters authentic?

> ➤ Would it improve my story to add colloquialism, a more informal manner of speaking, or a habitual sentence or phrase that the characters could be counted on to say?

> ➤ Do my characters speak with dialects that I would like to use to honor the region or country from which they hail?

When you're building scenes and giving fine touches, tell it like it is, and rewrite until "you're blue in the face," if that's what it takes. Even the prolific and accomplished Toni Morrison says she sometimes writes a single sentence a hundred times— perhaps that is one of the many reasons she is a bestselling author. *TellTale Soul* Jarvis could not, for the life of her, choose just one mother to write about when I interviewed her. *Haute Couture* was shaped by a composite of mothers and scenes that melded times, localities, and voices to produce a woman who was unstoppable.

Haute Couture

~Jarvis Jones

Oh Lordy, I had so many mothers. I wouldn't want to choose a memory of just one. The power of what they had to teach, of what each gave to me is absolutely interrelated spiritually. What they all had in common, what drew me even to the ones who were not of my family (not by blood, anyway) was that they all loved people and they all loved life, every morsel of it. Each mother was exciting in her own way, but each was different, too.

Combining my mothers into a composite picture, paying no mind to which culture each was from, I discover there are more similarities than differences in the human soul. This and the feeling that people are basically interconnected and it's love that binds us together are what I keep in front of me as I live my life.

Growing up on my grandparents' farm, filled with extended family, I was insulated from the larger world by the love of three generations. Surrounded by fields of heavy-headed sunflowers, the sultry scent of deep pit barbecue, the lazy flicking of a pony's tail attending to a fly, I flourished. With the American blend of Indian and African from my Grandpapa Charlie and Grandmama Lutecia came a reverence and respect for all of life and a strong faith in the Lord. By this spirit they raised their children and helped so many people. But this being Canton, Mississippi, I learned in the 1960s that all of life was not so tranquil.

Especially in times of strife or injustice, Grandmama Lutecia's teachings came in real handy. She taught that religion is something private between me and the Lord, you and the Lord, and her and the Lord, and that prayer is the way to reach the Lord. But prayer in a meditative way, so as to develop an individual relationship with the Lord. At times, Grandmama would just send us out yonder on the land by ourselves so we could meditate and pray. There was a lot of ground to wander. I think each of us had a special place. She'd coached us on the distinctive qualities found in the stillness of the woods, the murmuring of a creek, the solidness of a flattop boulder. Any time we were troubled, she'd send us away to be by ourselves in this way, with only the Lord as our guide. Sending us away didn't necessarily mean far, just any place where we could concentrate enough to go deep inside and tune out the outside world. That place might only be the lower step on the porch or the bench out back by the pump. It didn't matter so long as you came away feeling better than when you went, with some peace of mind.

I learned from Grandmama that peace of mind comes from release and acceptance of whatever may "a been troublin'"; not especially an answer to my problems or the way I might wish for things to be, just acceptance for the ways things are after I put myself in the Lord's hands. The point is to just let go. It does no good to try holding onto something that I can't change.

This meditative prayer was a natural part of our lives that we learned from Grandmama back then, before it became a big thing. I've used what she taught throughout my life, and I've found it works for personal relationships and business, too.

When I was coming up, my mother made most of my clothes by hand, using only a needle and thread—wonderful pleated skirts, dresses with plackets, and blouses with scalloped collars that she'd find pictured in magazines. Although I never paid much mind as a child to Mama's sewing, I had a flair for fashion, a good eye, and a lot of nerve mixed with a great belief in myself from Grandmama Lutecia's introspective training.

So armed with Mama's flair and Grandmama's confidence, I put myself out as a designer in Milwaukee in the company of some shrewd friends, with a bundle of business sense, who not only believed in me but also pulled me into the fertile bosom of Jewish tradition and culture.

My office quickly became cluttered with the latest designs by Yves St. Laurent, Christian Dior, and Perry Ellis. My new clients wanted knock-offs! I sweated bullets, buckets of bullets, but I wasn't scared. I never felt like I couldn't do it. I trained myself to sit at my desk, my office brimming with all kinds of folks and chatter clattering off the walls, and go deep inside myself to pray to the Lord or talk to Grandmama or Mama. Those around me didn't know what I was doing – I wasn't praying out loud. If my designs didn't come out just so, I'd just have to accept it, by God, and my clients would have to accept it, too.

At first, I had no idea what to do or where to begin. Nothing comes until I start going inside and praying. In a silent, "inside" connection with my mother, I says, "Mama, how do I make a sleeve, an armhole?" She looks me square in my mind's eye and guides me with the best advice I've ever had, "Well, ya jes looks at it, Baby Rose, and ya jes draws it and ya jes do it."

That simple little thing my mama told me was all I needed. My great lesson in life is this: If someone else could, then I could, too. If Yves St. Laurent could put that sucker together, nothing's stopping me. I might have to pray a week or more before the insight comes and I get a release and produce. But it has never happened that nothing came.

Photo contributed by Jarvis: My Grandmama and Grandpapa

Jarvis Jones: "Thank you, Lynn, for being a mother to my daughter, Dominique. When you wrote my story after taping me telling it to you, you tapped into the essence of my spirit and captured my inner consciousness. My gift as a haute couture designer was passed down to me from my mother, my grandmother, and my great grandmother."

WRITE: First read your story as though you were hearing it for the first time, while keeping the following questions in mind.

Does this story grab my attention?

Are my scenes strong?

Did I infuse it with essential energy?

Does each voice ring true?

Did I add sparks to enliven the details of personalities and events?

Have I created passion and emotion?

Did I use my imagination, while maintaining truth?

Did I leave out elements essential to the story line?

Then rework your bio-vignette until you feel good about what you have written and your work reflects truth and understanding.

I believe in a coming together of spirits between daughters and sons with their individual mothers as they write the *Mother Memoir*. And I believe an ever widening circle forms around people from all walks of life as stories are shared and embraced for sheer universality of emotion.

One voice can carry a note, two voices join in harmony, many voices does a choir make. One story can be told, two stories share rapport, many stories does a woman make.

It's the mingling of our stories and the melding of our shared experiences that renew us and complete us as human beings. Embracing one another other is a choice; one made naturally when we take the time to hear the fullness of our voices raised together. All it takes is a reminder, an inner chord struck lightly, to awaken the echoes of stored memory that join one soul with the next. Narrowing the space between us allows us to embrace on an intuitive level. To jump barriers. To float across boundaries. Our life tales are seen as earthy by some and, by others, as territory of the gods.

Memories dance like ghosts in our heads until we realize we have the power to set them free. I wrote the following poem some years ago in honor of would-be writers of the *Mother Memoir* hesitant to take first steps into writing their telling tales.

GHOST DANCE

I crept inside and found you
oh ghosts of persistent passion,
sacred dancers, anticipating me;
chant-like voices calling, cries summoning—
seeking communion...

Concentric rings of shadows embrace,
spirits soar united, receiving, awakening,
inscribing one more soul, ghost dance resumes;
mothers, sisters, daughters, the throng consumes—
we nod in recognition...

I chose the ethereal path seeking you, and
found ageless, fervid wisdom, thick liquid;
otherworldly things now manifest in core.
children of grace, voiceless ones, my time to guide
your dance...

All ghosts of mothers, burgeoning with radiance;
spirit flames now molten sterling strokes on canvas;
hands molding clay, forever blending, bending, gushing—
releasing memories encoded in repose, etched in seed—for you
progeny.

As each flower has its day in the sun, so must it fade, returning to the earth and to seed, making way for the miraculous unfolding of the next in line. So it is with all mothers.

Our hopes and dreams for our children are that they will be stronger, more intelligent, have greater health and beauty than we, and live in a world more compassionate than one we leave for them. In the rich soil of our collective soul the seeds of unity and joy await our exploration.

Let's take steps across the garden, you and I together, to weave garlands from shared wisdom. Let's come close and celebrate new vision from the old, and set again our soaring souls to hear the full flower of woman unfurl.

Lynn Cook Henriksen

We spend lifetimes seeking answers to life's biggest questions and striving to arrive at our ideal destinations, only to find that there are neither answers nor destinations—only journeys.

Act Five

Who are we without memory? Who are we without memoir? What is life, anyway, without stories? Does life make sense if not filled with tales that tell us from whence we came? When it comes right down to it, stories are all we have; they are the foundation that supports us until the curtain falls on the final act of our lives. Stories not only shape our lives, they also guide each of us toward living a life filled with greater wisdom and universal understanding.

Throughout Act Five, we will contemplate the results of walking the memoir labyrinth, consciously connect, celebrate the wonder of story and voice, and realize the ultimate value in the sharing of our gifts. This will be the time for you to grace the stage, front and center, to take that final bow; although, please realize when the curtain closes—hold on—your journey will have only just begun. Beginnings are born by successfully integrating the echoes of the past with truth and vision through the act of writing.

WALKING THE MEMOIR LABYRINTH

I see walking a labyrinth as a metaphor for the passionate journey we are traveling into memoir writing. Labyrinths have been with us for centuries and have been used by folks in many parts of the world as a path on their spiritual quests or for exploring aspects of their lives in a thoughtful manner. Labyrinths are beautiful, intricate structures that appear to have sacred qualities ascribed to them. Yet, they are uncomplicated and undemanding when the simple act of walking slowly and mindfully through them to the center and back out again is used as a meditative process to search inwardly.

When I helped you locate memories, we did an *innersearch* in a less formal, less structured way than walking through a classic labyrinth. I asked you to explore the deepest recesses of your mind to locate buried treasure in relationship to your mother as you prepared to write your bio-vignette. Whether what appeared during reflective time was an image, a sign, the fleeting sound of music, a voice, a searing pain, or a belly laugh, the memories that surfaced did so for a reason. Only you, as the writer, held the power to find the explanations and your personal truths for what you found through this exercise. The results of your discovery took into consideration intuitive interpretation as well as creative license.

In a way similar to walking the memoir labyrinth, the time you spent writing about an emotionally charged memory, which you used as the basis for your *Mother Memoir*, was also fraught with hesitations at various turns. There were choices to be made along the writing path that only you, the writer and creator of the story, could resolve. It was through the very act of writing that the emotional hold each memory had on you was revealed. By writing through your feelings with understanding and passion, a certain momentum built until you were propelled to craft that *one* original, true and telling tale that would capture your mother's character and keep her spirit alive for generations to come.

Stories guide our way through life no matter place or stage. I trust you are finding this experience a valuable spiritual quest and a reliably mindful journey. Looking at the essence of mother through the lens of compassionate understand and finding wisdom by walking the labyrinth, allowed you to connect not only with your mother, but also with the many mothers gathered together in this book.

I have often heard *TellTale Souls* remark that they felt so good about what they had accomplished by taking steps into the wide and wonderful world of *Mother Memoir* that they intended to expand their powerful scenes into a book-length memoir or write a novel. Remember, your first true tale may be a beginning. One woman, with whom I worked, became so inspired she sold her business, applied for a grant, and she is now fervently working on her first novel. She wrote a beautiful story during the course of my class, so I have no doubt one day I will be browsing in a bookstore when I catch her winking at me from an upfront display of new and exciting works.

Your story will inspire, just as you have been inspired by stories written by other *TellTale Souls*. Please take some time to revel in the fact that you have successfully written, or are coming close to finishing, a compelling bio-vignette. This is a first for many of you, so take a bow. You deserve a standing ovation. Celebrate the fact that you are using your unique voice to keep your mother's spirit alive. I have often been on the scene when *TellTale Souls* experience the thrill of completing what they set out to do. It is exhilarating for me, too, to be there as they grasp the reality of how much more fully they see their mothers, as well as themselves, after this intense experience.

Now to take this process one step further, I encourage you to consider inviting the spirit of your mother to join you in an *innersearch*, if doing so feels comfortable, since journeying together is a means of bringing more stored information to the surface, and it can be an exhilarating experience. If you find this mother-daughter/mother-son *innersearch* personally fitting, even more secrets may be revealed as she travels with you into days gone by.

As you have previously done, on your journey throughout this book, find a comfortable sitting position, with pad and pencil near, and take a moment to think about your objective in seeking your mother's presence during this *innersearch*. Specifically call her name and invite her to join you in your own words.

- ➤ Consciously begin to exclude the outer world as you include your mother.
- ➤ Close your eyes slowly so that you are aware of the shades being drawn—your sight receding.
- ➤ Take a couple of slow, deep breaths and sink into the moment . . .
- ➤ As you exhale, breathe out all your mind chatter to allow yourself to move from exterior surroundings.
- ➤ Each time you deeply inhale, notice she is beside you.
- ➤ Breathe slowly in, slowly out, moving further inside, together with your mother, as you draw each breath.
- ➤ Allow mom's presence to give you additional sight, awareness, a new beginning.
- ➤ After several minutes, slowly open your eyes, thank your mother for joining you, and return to the here and now.

> **WRITE:** First, quickly note unusual insights, fleeting images, and emotions you became aware of during this joint *innersearch* with your mother. Now write one page expressing, in depth, the feelings this exercise brought forth.

You may need some time to sort out what you have learned and contemplate your feelings and emotions after this *innersearch*. You may or may not wish to include your new discoveries in your bio-vignette. You may want to keep what you have already written as is—complete in itself, or you may want to begin to write your second *Mother Memoir* based on where this new experience has taken you.

Prior to the telling of your tale, you may have spent a lifetime looking at mom in a certain way, possibly without really seeing *who* she is. Had you previously wondered who this woman is at her core? You are writing a story to pay tribute to her soul, honor your relationship, or better understand her, but, beyond that, you have learned that your ultimate objective for writing this bio-vignette is to question your personal assumptions about her, in particular. Since your impressions of mother are keyed to your memory, don't make assumptions—about anyone, for that matter. True stories take shape and allow you to make sense of whom you are.

From here it follows that reading stories written from the heart by ordinary people is the best way to learn about others, since we are each connected, one to the next, at the root of our beings.

Who is each woman in her own right? How does she fit into the sea of womankind? What is the face of woman?

These are questions to continue to ask as you celebrate the personal experience of getting to know your mother in a more expansive way while venturing out to meet the mothers of others.

Finding new insights into the character of your mother and holding your findings out for other people to appreciate is the first step to consciously connecting to the soul-line. The second step is looking at womankind in a whole and conscious way, which we will investigate in the *Consciously Connecting* section ahead, just after you take an inquisitive pause with Mom over the next few pages....

REALIZING THERE'S MORE THAN MEETS THE EYE

The unobserving, untrained eye, that is. By now you are practiced in observing your subject fully. You didn't want to leave a stone unturned. You looked beneath the surface and mindfully surveyed your mother's character and spirit and the setting for your story using all of your senses, topped with creative imagination and imbued with the insight intuition allows. Perhaps, in search of truth, you purposely slipped into your subconscious mind hand-in-hand with your mother during that special *innersearch* outlined in the last section.

One of world's most celebrated French authors of the past century is perhaps best known by her surname, Colette. I mention Sidonie-Gabrielle Colette again because she wrote often and in depth about her mother and some of her succinct, descriptive prose is inspiring. The incomparable beauty in the following quote describing her mother, Sido, bears repeating, *"She had a curious way of lifting roses by the chin to look them full in the face."*

> ➤ How do you feel about this sentence?
> ➤ What does it say to you?

Lift your mother's chin, if only in thought, and look her full in the face. Go out into a garden, find a rose, and gaze into its depths and wonder at its intricacy and strength, its scent. Look at it in a natural light, but be wary of its thorn and know that without just the right amount of sun and water and nutrients it would not be a thing of beauty. Whether your rose is a little misshapen, touched with mold and mildew, a host for pests, or whether it is bold, radiant, and clear, the essence of its perfume is unmistakable.

Pause and ask yourself:

➤ Did I look for truth in all the right places?
➤ Have I viewed things from her vantage point?
➤ Are there alternative ways of seeing her?

Know that there are alternative ways of looking at her. Ask: WHO IS this woman I call mother? Look at your mother as you would imagine her as a little girl. What if she were your little girl?

➤ *What* were her hopes and dreams, her tragedies and sorrows?
➤ *When* did she become fulfilled; *when* did she turn bitter; *when* did she stop believing in herself; *when* did love and hope triumph?
➤ *Where* did her life's journey take her; *where* did she win or *where* did she fail; where does she fit into the scheme of life, the sisterhood of woman?
➤ *Why* did she make the choices she made?
➤ *How* do you think she feels or felt about her life?

As I collected stories from *TellTale Souls* over the years, I decided one day to write down my feelings connecting Mom to the work she inspired me to do. The following, is not my bio-vignette, but it reflects a few brief thoughts at the time:

Mulling over how I think about my mother after teaching others to write the Mother Memoir *was a heady experience. First Mom's memory and then her life gave way to the insidious disease that is Alzheimer's, but her spirit lives on. She was the stimulus that spawned my work, paying tribute to the soul of woman. It was fitting: Her horizons were expansive, her mind open, as she embraced most everything and everybody with gusto and gave of herself unselfishly. I'd say she often had "a tough row to hoe" in her adult life, but she didn't dwell on the hardships. Mom said to me years ago, "You know, I don't remember the bad things that happened to me. I just remember the good things. It's a great life!" Back then, I considered Mom an ostrich for sticking her head in the sand, for not confronting issues which were hers, but things I thought needed attention. I no longer feel that way. Who was I to reproach her for looking at life her way?*

How does it feel to know her—your mother—as an individual? In the telling tale below, Louise's story begins over 100 years ago, but upon reading it today you can trace the feelings of hope, love, duty, honor, and compassion through a thread of authenticity stretching from her mother's childhood through that of Louise's own.

Bubbles

~Louise Rood

*T*he year was 1910. It was time for her to put away her childhood and become an adult. She bid farewell to her large and loving family in her native Poland (which was part of Russia then). She was sixteen when the ship, The Vaterland, passed the Statue of Liberty, symbol of hope and the new life awaiting her.*

Bubbles was a nickname awarded her as a child. She was full of high spirits, a little girl not to be contained. The girl who had stolen the coins used to balance the scales in her father's store, the imp who scared the wits out of her mother when she rode up six stories to the top floor of a building hidden in a mattress that movers were delivering by pulley, the rebel who read Emile Zola's NANA secretly under the sheets, she would choose not to put her nickname behind her. Too much love was contained in it.

In this new land of opportunity, Bubbles spent three years in nurse's training, one of the few positions open to women, and became a registered nurse. America was a great land of opportunity for anyone who wanted to work hard, but for her, it wasn't one of luxury. She found a job in the lower East Side neighborhood where she lived in a tenement with an uncle, aunt, and cousins making umbrellas in a sweatshop to contribute to the family expenses and put herself through school.

Before her life became settled, she did her part to support her new nation and the principles in which she believed. When the United States entered the First World War, she joined the Red Cross and was transferred into the U.S. Nurse Corps. From there, she was sent to France. Again and again, while nursing the wounded at the field hospitals in eastern France, Bubbles' effervescent spirit rose to the surface in displays of irrepressible compassion. More than once she got into trouble with her superiors for treating injured German prisoners with the same humanity with which she treated our own men. She was stubborn in doing what she thought was right.

In Paris before the war ended, Bubbles fell in love with a shy, handsome soldier in the U.S. Army Corp of Engineers. They returned to New York, it was home for both of them, but home on different levels for each. Her future husband's family had been in this country for several generations—the uptown Jews didn't mix with the downtown Jews. At that time, the older, established German Jews looked down their noses at the uncultured Eastern European greenhorns, except for the occasional excursions into "social work." This didn't make much sense to Bubbles, who was bursting with light, conceiving a world full of truth, fairness, and promise. She rose above the snobbery, holding no animosity toward her future in-laws, promptly married her true love, and began to raise a family within the year.

She mothered me with this same veracity. I remember an expression my mother used as she ripped the adhesive plaster off the scrapes and bruises of my active childhood. I complained tearfully, "Ouch, that hurts."

And she replied, "Funny, I don't feel a thing." Bubbles was a loving and compassionate mother, so I knew she was trying to make me laugh as she did what was necessary.

In the late 1940s, I remember expressing deep anguish to Mama over the political rubbish being generated by the McCarthy hearings. Each day the newspaper headlines got scarier and scarier, and I feared the era of the Bill of Rights and all free speech was to end forever. But Mama reminded me that she lived with memories of rioting and the burning of Black neighborhoods, of the beatings of German-Americans during the First

World War, of the Great Depression, the worker unions' bloody struggles, the genocide and mass killings by the Nazis, the internment in this country of the Japanese, and many more dark events. She comforted me by presenting the resilience of the human spirit and the inevitability of the swinging pendulum of history. I still take comfort in those words.

And she was my greatest defender when, as a child, I became a "cause celebre" in our neighborhood.

Time moves in a continuous flow for a child, so I don't remember our ages exactly or how long we had speculated on where exactly babies came from. But I know my knowledge extended further than the "stork" or the "cabbage patch" or even "at the hospital," answers my best friend, Olga, had been given.

It was a warm summer day, Olga and I were out on the little wooden porch just off the side of her house with most of the world, as we knew it, spread out flatly before us. An ocean breeze may have been blowing in from lower New York Bay just a few yards and a beach width away. We could see the two-seater airplanes land and take off again as they patrolled the harbor. The skies were the blue of a perfect day as we assembled our dolls and makeshift doll beds, highchairs, and buggies. In our innocence, we assumed no one was listening and the world was ours alone.

The question of babies came up again. And this time I had an answer. I had been figuring things out and questioning my mother. I had not been fed a diet of fairy tales and lies, and Mama did not hide information from me if I had the maturity to ask. Mama had verified my hunch that somehow mommies and daddies were both involved in the baby-making process, that the "action" took place in the bed that they shared, and that the baby grew from a seed in the mother's stomach. Luckily for Mama, exactly how the seed got there was not something I wondered about. And I was convinced that babies were born out of the belly button, because I couldn't imagine any other solution, so I hadn't even questioned Mama about that.

As Olga and I sat that day in the warm sunshine in our own little world playing house, I proceeded to happily share my information and misinformation with her about where babies came from, belly-button-birth and all. But we weren't out of earshot of Olga's mother—a good and loving woman, but not so progressive and liberated as Mama.

Our play was abruptly interrupted. I was sent home for the afternoon, completely unaware of any wrong-doing on my part. Our community must have been full of gossip. I found out years later that Mama received a lot of criticism from other parents for allowing me knowledge, which in my innocence, I had indiscriminately made public. But Mama protected me from the worst aspects of our neighborhood, bearing the criticism herself.

I realize today parts of life in our community must have been stifling for Bubbles. I also understand that most of the attitudes I call my own I learned from Mama. I wish I could tell her how grateful I am to her for helping me form the parts of myself I like best.

Louise Rood: "After I retired as a volunteer, working five nights a week at the Men's Homeless Shelter in Brooklyn, I realized my greatest satisfaction came from making a difference in someone's life, if only for one night."

We have discussed, among other things, truth and honesty, but what are those concepts in actuality? I think the answer is found by looking at all sides of each woman from her backstory clear through to the vantage point of today. Had you ever stopped to look at your mother as a woman unto herself prior to writing your short, true tale? Were you surprised by what you saw? Do you find it easy or difficult to really see her in her own right? Take a good long reflective break from the well-formed picture you have of your mother and look at her as an individual.

WRITE: Fill up as many lines or pages as you choose as you look back on your mother's life, as well as your own, now that you have explored alternate ways of looking at your mother from the inside out, walked the memoir labyrinth, and completed your telling tale.

CONNECTING CONSCIOUSLY

I mentioned the second step to connecting consciously is to look at other woman and their stories in an entirely new and completely conscious way. Once we desire to connect on a spiritual level with other human beings, a bond of intimacy is assured. Much like the act of tossing a pebble into a glassy lake, the ripple effect of our reaching out through understanding and true caring ever widens. I notice when I smile at people I don't know, a smile is more often than not returned. There is something basic in the human spirit that yearns for acceptance and love and comprehends what it feels like to be united.

WHAT IS THE FACE OF WOMAN?

Has that face changed for you since you began your journey to becoming a *TellTale Soul*? Do you now realize—had the circumstances of your birth been different—your mother could have been any woman in the world and you could be anyone's daughter or son on the face of the globe. We, as a people, will be entirely triumphant and successful when we embrace each soul we meet with awe and an interest in the mystery that surrounds him or her. Being able to consciously connect with people outside ourselves is the most valuable aid to understanding the richness of life, be that through personal interaction or the sharing of stories across continents.

Can you imagine a world in which everyone had someone look at them with sincerity and want to *know* who they are, what makes them tick? Don't we all feel the need to be understood, liked, even go so far as to say we want to be cherished? Don't we all think we have the right to be loved and cared for?

TellTale Soul Karen shows us the face of a woman who was waiting to be loved and knew how to love:

Young Girl from Finland

~Karen Braschuk

My mother was born in 1929 in Finland. Even now, I can tell that she was a beautiful child. With blonde hair, green eyes, beautiful cheekbones and a delightful laugh that brightened up any room, she was a living doll with so much potential for happiness. She wasn't only physically attractive; she had the personality to match. She was simply a child waiting to be loved.

But we all know how real life gets in the way. Her parents had to ship her out to the countryside to live with her grandparents while they dealt with running their own business and the impending doom of WW2. It was not a cool time to be in Europe between 1935 and 1945.

Her father died in 1940 as a Finnish soldier during the early part of WW2. Her older sister, who had remained at home, had become a stranger. For all intents and purposes, when she was finally brought back home, she was greeted by a mother and a sister she barely knew, as well as no father. She was a lost soul who missed her grandparents and didn't want to be with these strangers, even though they were her very own mother and sister.

As her daughter, and hoping to revive at least one positive memory from her youth, I asked about her earliest memory of Christmas as a young child. To paraphrase my mother, she essentially said, "I remember receiving this gift of a doll that was made up of plastic or something like that. I remember walking too close to the Christmas tree with lit candles on it and then the doll bursting into flames. It was the only present I had and it was ruined in an instant."

Watching the emotion on my mother's face while she retold this story, noticing the pain in her eyes while she described how her doll had burned up and seeing her face revert to a young child's expression of horror and dismay made me want to cry. How awful that a young child should have to deal with that, especially since it was her only present.

Fast forwarding quite a few years, this very same young girl from Finland, who was given so little in terms of emotional support during her own childhood and grew up in a time of fear, war, deprivation and uncertainty, still found it in her heart to give the best of the best to her own children.

As I was growing up with my younger brother, I remember my mother doing so many kind things for us. As she was a seamstress, she would painstakingly create little perfect outfits for my Barbie doll—I had the best-dressed Barbie in town! She was always hardworking; if she wasn't selling cosmetics or Fuller brushes from door to door, she was spending tireless hours doing alterations and creating outfits for her ever-growing customer base. She truly was one of the pioneers in the world of home-based businesses.

As the years went by and I became a teenager, I always knew that whenever I had a fight with my boyfriend, an unrequited crush on someone, or a bad experience at school, I could sit at the edge of her bed for hours, talking and crying and sharing the angst of being an adolescent. She would put her book down and listen intently to every word I had to say. She would offer advice in her kind, gentle way and never let on how tired she was or how much she was truly looking forward to reading her book as an escape from her own sometimes difficult and wearying life. In short, she always had time for her daughter…always.

Many people who had been as neglected and emotionally deprived of love as she had been in her childhood might have turned bitter and unloving themselves. Not my mother. In fact, it's almost as if she vowed to never let her own children suffer the way she did. She turned a negative into a positive and had a never-ending supply of patience, empathy and love which she showed us each and every day. For that, I can only thank her for having the strength to see beyond her own pain to help me with my own struggles. My biggest desire is to be just as good a mom to my own children as that 'young girl from Finland' has always been to me.

You taught me well. I love you, Mom.

Photo of Karen contributed by Karen: Karen reflecting on Mom's wisdom.

Karen Braschuk: "To this day, my mother guides me with her wisdom and encourages me to always trust my 'gut' when it comes to relationships, everyday life, business decisions, and my own abilities (and my limitations). As the years go by, she appears wiser and wiser to me…or perhaps it is just me who has finally become wiser and more cognizant of what she has been teaching me all along simply by the way she has lived her own life."

THINK about the wisdom your mother imparted to you through her actions and the guidance you received from her. First make a list of the things you remember, and then WRITE a paragraph detailing the specifics of each item on your list.

*A woman writing thinks back
through all her mothers.*
~Virginia Woolf.

With Woolf's thought in mind and knowing it's a given that most travelers on this journey are women, I have written the following as you muse about consciously connecting woman-to-woman:

Dazzling and diverse are the three point three billion women alive today upon our Mother Earth. We all hum a familiar melody and dance to the music of the primal female soul. We utter words in thousands of languages and dialects and our skins radiate hundreds of shades and tones, but at the core we are connected through the single source of what it means to be Woman.

We share a common ancestry stemming from a common soul. No matter how great our differences appear, they pale in comparison to what we share. Our subconscious remembers all of our shared past; as science is now demonstrating, our very cells have memories that make the most advanced computer chips look like playthings.

How long has it been since you walked barefoot on a dusty trail, the sun warm upon your skin, without a worry on your mind? How long has it been since you let mud ooze between your toes at the edge of a creek bed and watched children splash in the cool waters? Some of us have never been so lucky, but if we go back far enough, we will find common ancestors who did walk those paths. Perhaps we have lost touch with the earth, with each other, and with the source of our female identity. We may be out of touch with the soul-line, but it is within our grasp.

We women are especially social creatures, ceaselessly striving to bind and bond. We nurture, we share, we have best friends, we gossip, cajole, and weep at inequity. In contrast, when we are out of sync with our true nature, we can be frighteningly treacherous and disdainful. We all laugh and cry in the same language. We make connections. We innately *feel* as we read the body language and nuances of those around us. We are great listeners.

Cradled in a primordial sea in a journey from conception to birth, each of us has listened to the steady beating of our own mother's heart. And deep within each mother the sounds of the ancient drumming of the collective female soul reverberate. While we may have strayed far from our common rooted connections, when we take the time to quiet ourselves, we can palpably feel the unmistakable vibrations of that drumbeat.

SHARING THE GIFTS OF STORY

We cannot help but connect when we hear other people's stories, whether that's by listening to stories being read aloud by someone we know, members of a group, or by reading intimate tales from a book such as this. The story tellers are sharing some of the most intimate parts of their lives with us—they are sharing their mothers with us.

When *TellTale Souls* bring together authentic, earthy stories celebrating the captured moments of a wide range of mothers, the overarching effect communicates the universality of the soul. "Aha! With her story I connect, in his story I see mine—ourstory." Familiarity is immediately felt through the sharing of stories even if the stories revolve around people very different from ourselves. Whether we connect primarily on a joyful level or whether we are empathizing with painful moments, the universal quality is unmistakable.

Our stories encompass the good and the bad, from stories that inspire to those that make us shudder. We wonder why anyone has to feel the pain of being mothered by a lost soul. There are reasons, but not good answers, as to why some women act cruelly, while others exude unselfish love. *TellTale Soul* Sharon's bio-vignette honors seemingly simple interactions between two women sharing moments where hearts and souls meet selflessly, while celebrating the joy of connecting and closing a door to grief through writing:

~~~ ∞ ~~~

Cups of Remembrance

~Sharon Walling

From the first cup of coffee we shared, my mother-in-law became my best friend. She used to call us and tell my husband, "You watch Daniel, and I'm going to fly Sharon up here for the weekend so we can go to "Music Circus." This was a series of off-Broadway productions. She loved music and concerts. We attended several together...always followed by dinner and conversation. Over French cuisine and good wine, she shared her deepest secrets with me, and her darkest regrets.

When she retired at 75 we brought her to live with us—healthy and happy. We have a guest apartment at the end of the hall. Frequently, I'd be marching down the hall with two cups of something to share with her, only to meet her carrying two cups...and we would laugh.

Less than a year later, she was diagnosed with cancer. We turned her room into a hospital room, replete with hospital bed, portable toilet, etc. Pancreatic cancer is a quick killer. She was becoming weaker and could no longer get out of bed.

I brought her a cup of water and remembered all the cups we had shared: the cup of laughter watching "Seven Brides for Seven Brothers"; the cup of excitement when she helped us purchase the house we would all live in; the cup of fear as we received her prognosis "you're going to die" from a disgruntled oncologist. But this night we would share a cup of tenderness.

My husband and son had gone to a movie. I picked up a John Michael Talbot tape "Come to the Quiet" and tiptoed into her room.

"Jeanne, are you awake?"

"Yes," she said, "I'm awake, why?"

"Well, since we can't go to a concert, we're going to have one here."

I put on the tape and climbed into bed with her. The soft guitar and soothing voice of John Michael brought the presence of the Holy Spirit and wrapped us together in peace. I held her like a mother cradles an infant.

As she looked up at me and smiled, I realized that this was not the end, but the beginning. Life as we know it is really the womb, and very soon she would be thrust into the light to begin her new life. This was our last concert together.

Sometimes when I miss her, I'll pick up a lovely cup that she gave me and drink my tea from the cup of remembrance, sweetened with hope and stirred with longing.

Photo contributed by Sharon Walling: My mother-in-law.

Sharon Walling: "I wrote Cups of Remembrance on the anniversary of my mother-in-law's passing. This short memoir closed the door on my grief and opened a gate to remember and honor a precious friendship."

Have you ever wondered if other women's stories are there to seek us out, to lead us to the discovery that we are at once one and all? I believe by sharing our stories all women and men will learn that there are, indeed, other ways of being. It is the mingling of our stories and the melding of our shared experiences that renew us and complete us. If we listen closely, we will hear the voices join until a soulful choir is born.

In the telling tale of my mother back in Act Three, where I merged thoughts, one line bears repeating, "If a soul can be heard, I imagine it would speak to me in just such a way as my mother's unconscious response on those occasions." I wrote that story long before I wrote this book; in fact, it was the predecessor for the entire collection of bio-vignettes. It is satisfying to realize that a smidgen—one of Mom's often used words—of my mother's soul stayed on for this ride, as we near the end of the journey through *Writing the Mother Memoir.*

Before we move into the final section of Act Five, I want to touch on some ideas for presenting and preserving your work: *Don't Let the Goblins Get Your* Work—and they will, no doubt, find it. Once you've completed your telling tale, you need to make sure it is presented in a manner that fits the bill—your play bill—and that it is protected from critters and the elements, so that sharing it now is gratifying, all the while ensuring that future generations will have the opportunity to experience your mother's individuality and spirit, just as they will appreciate your voice, your insight, and your will and power to make lasting connections.

Whether you wrap up your short, true tale, along with snapshots or other memorabilia, to give as a gift, or plan to store it in a cool, dark place away from pests, you will want to protect your work from time and environmental damage. Most of us are well aware of the unkind and unsympathetic tricks time plays on the human body—your body of work is not immune, be it only a few pages or a tome. And the elements, as well as human hands, are full of acidic little creatures waiting to digest or dissolve your memoirs.

I'm not suggesting securing the *Mother Memoir* in a bottle, corking it, and setting it free to be discovered someday, someway, by someone; although, we are told that method has worked, at least in fiction. But we are talking essential, creative narrative, so let's get serious and rely on nonfictional ideas.

Some papers and ink also fade over time, much like memory, and computer hard-drives crash—a quick, easy, and portable way to back up is to use a memory stick. It is fairly easy today to find acid-free writing and printing paper—even acid-free ink pens. Many laminating films and adhesives are manufactured to be pH neutral (7) in order to preserve and protect vital documents. Since this is not my area of expertise, make inquires at your local paper supply stores, copying services, and book stores for these items or go shopping for them online.

I'm reminding you to consider the significance in writing your story out in long-hand, since there is a quality of intimacy in this basic act that can't be accomplished by alternative means, like words processed by machines. I've had simple handwritten notes laminated because I cherish them and it would sadden me if they were ruined by the forces of Mother Nature.

If you want to publish your writing, there are also many publishers who use acid-free materials in the books they produce, although many don't—if you are concerned, ask them. Speaking of publishing, there are an enormous amount of options for getting your work published. In fact, a vast array of books dedicated entirely to publishing options line the shelves of bookstore and libraries, as well as all across the internet. The choices are dizzying, ever changing, evolving.

For most unrecognized authors, there are unlimited avenues to self-publishing. If you choose to take this path, I recommend working with an experienced editor prior to doing so. Since this is not my area of expertise, I will provide a brief overview into self-publishing, and from there you can research the options that interest you. Online, via the internet in ezines or posted on blogs (your site or someone else's), is a great way to get a story or two out into the world. Vanity presses can be worked with by contracting with an established company to print your work for a fee. Printer direct means going straight to a printing company and paying them per book or booklet to print books in any amount you request. Independent publishing means you will form an individual company to print and distribute your work at your discretion. eBooks, formatted as digital files, are listed for sale chiefly through online sources, then uploaded into applications to be read on eReader devices and other electronic appliances (much like iTunes works for music). Whatever the direction you decide to take, there are numerous resources to help you find what you are looking for. Be persistent.

Be faithful in small things because it is
in them that your strength lies.
~Mother Teresa

REFLECTING ON THE JOURNEY

There is the immediate side to the journey of discovery, which is the creation of your *Mother Memoir*, but it has far-reaching effects as well. The extent of your journey won't end abruptly by completing your story. You now carry wisdom and understanding on a deep level that has become integrated into your psyche, and it has a lasting impact on the awareness you have of yourself, your mother, and other women throughout the world.

We, as *TellTale Souls*, find ourselves drawn in, craving more. Not only do we wish to experience more insight into the people significant in our own lives, but we also want to know the secrets of people from different walks of life. Most of us have an insatiable curiosity about other people and their stories. It is as though, like Alice visiting Wonderland, we yearn to find the key to where the magic of the soul is kept. We found the key to open memories of our own, and now we realize this journey opens directly into the intimate force of other people's stories.

Women innately like to share knowledge and wisdom; a vital step to accomplishing this connection is by reaching out through deceptively simple telling tales. The light emanating from our stories radiates with universal insight, awareness, and true caring until the resulting expansiveness overlaps the delicate sphere of the next story and the next—the concentric circle ever widens.

I believe it is important to celebrate success, not simply move on without clinking the glass and taking a sip to salute your achievements. Looking back over your travels so far through the world of the *Mother Memoir* will give you the precious time and space to revel in the significance of what you have accomplished through writing your bio-vignette as well as taking to heart the stories of other people. I trust you have come to the point where you realize with certainty that the melding of our souls through story has only just begun.

We experience our finest hours traveling the river of the soul where we find that stream of consciousness that binds us together rather than tears us apart. Although we may hold conflicting thoughts and memories when we think of our mothers, SHE has been, in reality, our muse throughout— imagine, we may have actually thought we had done it by ourselves!

WRITE a page capturing the spiritual dimension of your relationship with your mother.

In the end, when one's mother's voice is only a memory, even for—perhaps especially for—those who wished for a better relationship, it brings up a sadness and a longing that is indescribable. For years, I reflexively, futilely reached for the phone to call my mother. Oh, what I'd give to have her grace my doorway for one more day, to feel our arms around each other one more time! This brings me to a story a woman told me some time ago that she said she'd never told anyone else: For a very long time after her mother passed away, she'd often dial her mother's phone number to listen to the piercing ringing permeate the terrible silence at the other end of the line—the silence that had replaced the reliability and comfort of her mother's voice.

We are, each of us, a gift to one another. We have so much to give, so much to learn, and so much to share by adventuring down the path of story. Our stories fill a void, link our spirits, and reenergize our souls as they illuminate universal connections and provide greater awareness of whom we are. We spring from the same core, so, as a whole, we can be greater than the sum of our parts. It is plain to see how disastrous it is for us as a people to allow race to be pitted against race and to have mother pitted against child in political or psychological games. We don't grow, we cannot love fully, when we place blame rather than take today as our own and make a clear tomorrow our choice. Our future dazzles, it delights, when we honor the path to the soul-line.

We spend lifetimes seeking answers to life's biggest questions and striving to arrive at our ideal destinations, only to find that there are neither answers nor destinations—only journeys, journeys of discovery where the self is mirrored in another woman's eyes, encountered in her story, or understood through spiritual reflections that unmistakably anchor us to our source. *"She pulled in her horizon like a great fish-net. Pulled it from around the waist of the world and draped it over her shoulder. So much of life in its meshes! She called in her soul to come and see."* Moving us beyond words, the depth and meaning of this passage by Zora Neale Hurston illuminates the path. The external dimensions of our daily lives are what we must deal with in the here-and-now, but it is in recognizing shared experience and wordless knowledge called up from within that we begin to live lives filled with empathy, forgiveness, genuine care, grace, and satisfaction.

My personal awakening, my realization of our relatedness as women, regardless of our backgrounds goes like this: *She gazed out at me from worlds away without a whisper crossing her lips; she spoke to me in the single language that lives in mothers' souls. Baby at my breast, TV tuned to the news, I sat comfortably on the sofa watching my daughter's peachy cheeks work eagerly at nursing. I glanced up to find a disconcerting picture filling the television screen—a picture of a mother holding her child to her breast. She and I connected for mere seconds, seconds that spanned eternity and ruptured my complacent consciousness. That mother's eyes penetrated my being: her story, one of devastation and resignation as famine and draught claimed hundreds of thousands of lives in sub-Saharan Africa. Her baby was emaciated, skin taut over ribs where I could imagine the gleam of pearly bone through nut-brown skin. His huge-seeming head hung against her deflated, dusty breasts, while vacant eyes at half-mast drew flies. She had little to offer her baby but encircling arms until death. Chills crawled across my skin and tears from deep inside slid from my eyes as I pulled my baby closer. I had "called in my soul to come and see." I knew she loved her baby as much as I loved mine. We were in essence one in the same.*

Whether out of sorrow and tragedy or happiness and delight, whether through intimate relationships or a touch that spans continents, we will find if we simply listen that we share the soul of that mother and child I described above. This knowledge awaits us as we continue on our journeys.

The voices set free by writing and sharing the *Mother Memoir*—their idiosyncrasies and their dance—inspire. Looking at each woman *full in the face* with an inquisitive eye and a touch of respect releases the fragrant scent of her soul. The women alive in the stories are and were motivated by circumstances unique to each, but their roots grow deep and are fed by a single spring that is clear and certain. In full bloom they are a spectacular sight. And each new story, added by a *TellTale Soul*, widens the avenue for richer respect and deeper admiration for womankind, as we connect through strength, energy, and creativity. To the collective voice I say, "Hurray! It was my pleasure to have met you, to have learned from you, to have honored you. Your spirits dazzle."

WRITE: Take quality time right now to write about where this journey into the *Mother Memoir* has taken you and what this experience has meant to you and to those around you.

CALL FOR RESPONSES AND STORIES

Now it's your turn to guide me.

I would enjoy receiving your responses to the questions below that you find pertinent:

- ➢ What did it mean to you to write your bio-vignette?
- ➢ What were the most important ideas you took away from this guidebook?
- ➢ What were the Aha! moments or breakthroughs you experienced?
- ➢ Did you come away with more self-realization and understanding or appreciation of others, as well as yourself?
- ➢ Do you now have a better understanding of what you need to do to write a bio-vignette that contains energy, passion, and honesty?
- ➢ Were you inspired to connect with others through story?
- ➢ Why do you think it is important to write true tales about people who hold significance in your life?
- ➢ How do you see the memoir you wrote as a gift?
- ➢ Was there something you'd like to know about writing memoir that wasn't covered in the guidebook?
- ➢ Did you appreciate the bio-vignettes written by *TellTale Souls* that were interspersed throughout the book?
- ➢ Did you find universal connections?

I look forward to your feedback, since I value learning from you. Please click "Contact/About" on the menu bar of my website (www.telltalesouls.com) and blog to get in touch with me.

Call for stories:

I would also enjoy reading your completed, polished stories of mothers and others and perhaps include them in a subsequent volume of *TellTale Souls* or publish them on *The Story Woman* blog.

On the website you will find interesting, motivating information, as well as submission guidelines and the portal through which to submit your telling tale—click "Submit Your Story" on the menu bar. When you submit your story (www.telltalesouls.com), please make sure you include your email address so that I can contact you.

GLOSSARY

Quick Reference of Literary Terms and Devices for *TellTale Souls*—

Action: The energetic use of the details of conflicts and events that enliven the plot and make a story engaging.

Alliteration: A literary device where you use repetition of the initial consonant sounds in two or more words in a sentence or phrase.

Anecdote: A short interesting or humorous account of an incident.

Autobiography: Your account or story of your own life.

Backstory: A helpful tool to gain insight from the gathering of information that molded a character's life.

Biography: Your written account or story of someone else's life.

Bio-vignette: Your short, descriptive story capturing the character and spirit of someone who had a significant impact upon your life.

Catharsis: A psychological release brought about after bringing repressed emotions and feelings to the surface in an effort to identify and come to grips with them.

Character: The distinguishing features, attributes, disposition, and qualities of a person, place, or thing.

Character sketch: Writing in which you reveal and portray important aspects or distinguishing features of an individual.

Characterization: The method you use to reveal or describe the actions and personalities of your characters.

Climax: The point of greatest intensity or power in your story.

Colloquialism: Characteristics of informal speech and writing used conversationally. Expressions you remember used by folks in your locality.

Conflict: A clash, problem, or struggle in your story that triggers the action.

Context: The circumstances or set of facts around which an event or situation occurs in your story.

Critique: A form of constructive feedback, critical assessment, comment, or review.

Dialogue: A conversational passage of words between two or more characters in your tale.

Empathy: Identification with and understanding of the thoughts or feelings of another person—imagining yourself in someone else's shoes.

Emotional Memory: Intrinsic memory heightened by the emotions attached to them as they were stored. Emotional memories carry the greatest charge, rendering them more valuable to your inner psyche.

Exaggeration: To represent as greater than is actually the case—when you stretch the truth for dramatic effect.

Fiction: Literary works based on imagination, not necessarily on facts.

Flashback: An interruption in your story depicting an earlier incident for the purpose of making something in the present more clearly realized.

Free-write: Writing non-stop with a focus on your mother's character, a specific memory, or your feelings regarding your telling tale.

Foreshadowing: To indicate, give clues, and hint about what is to come later in your story.

Genre: A particular type or category of literature that is based on its style, form, and content. The story you write about your mother is categorized as memoir.

Hyperbole: A figure of speech that you would use to exaggerate or overstate a situation, event, or characteristic.

Imagery: Vivid words or phrases you select to create certain pictures in the reader's mind, usually based on sensory details.